Joan Squelch

PARENT PARTICIPATION

HOW TO HELP YOUR CHILD SUCCEED AT SCHOOL

ACACIA

Acacia Books, Reg. No. 05/11749/06
Division of the National Educational Group
1064 Arcadia Street, Hatfield
P.O. Box 151, Pretoria, 0001
Typography by Acacia Books
Cover design by A. Amien
Set in 11 on 12 pt Plantin
Lithographed and bound by National Book Printers
Goodwood

ISBN 0 86817 117 4

First Edition
First Impression – March 1994

R29,80

THE BEST INTEREST OF THE
CHILD SHALL BE THE GUIDING
PRINCIPLE OF THOSE RESPONSIBLE
FOR HIS/HER EDUCATION AND
GUIDANCE. THAT RESPONSIBILITY
LIES IN THE FIRST PLACE WITH
HIS/HER PARENTS.

*The United Nations Declaration
of the Rights of the Child (1959)*

Acknowledgements

I wish to thank the following people for their valuable support:

Anne Goodrich for her insightful ideas, suggestions and comments.

Gillian Garrard for her interest and for assisting me with my research.

Deborah Taggart for her valuable assistance.

Dave Quail, Headmaster of Jeppe High School for Boys, for his valuable advice and for helping me to obtain information.

Andrew, my husband, for his continued support and encouragement throughout the project, and for helping me to prepare the manuscript for publication.

Contents

Preface
Introduction

PART I: KNOW YOUR CHILD'S SCHOOL

1 Parental rights and responsibilities in education
2 How schools work
3 Choosing the right school
4 The school curriculum
5 Examinations
6 Records and reports
7 Extracurricular activities
8 School trips and transport
9 Financial matters
10 Discipline and punishment
11 Parents as partners
12 Effective communication with the school
13 Getting the most out of parent-teacher meetings
14 Children with special needs
15 Medical matters

PART II: HELPING YOUR CHILD AT HOME

16 Motivating your child
17 Supporting discipline
18 Homework without tears
19 Helpful study hints
20 How to improve your child's reading and writing skills

Appendix A: Useful addresses
Reproducible pages
Bibliography
Index

Index

absenteeism 58
addresses 99

bursary 46

cards 57
class committees 53
communication 56
compulsory educa-
    tion 3
consent 41
contracts 18, 35
curriculum 4, 21, 22

discipline 47, 81
dental services 72
documents 17
duty 3

education, sex 25
education, physical 25
education, religious 24
examinations 27
extracurricular 37
extra tuition 69

fees 45

gifted 68
governing body 9, 51
governor 51

home visits 60
homework 83
homework, contract 86
immunisation 72

indemnity 42
insurance 43
interview 16
involvement 8

journeys 44

letters 58, 59

medical aid 39
medication 39
meetings 61
motivation 75

notes 57

open days 14

parents'
    association 52
praise 76
promotion 26
prospectus 14
punishment 47
punishment, corpo-
    ral 48, 80

reading 94
records 29, 30
reports 30
rewards 82
rights 3, 29
rules 47, 81
safety 38, 41
schools, types 11
self-esteem 75

study 89
study skills 90
subject choice 23
subsidy 45
supervision 38, 41,
    90
suspension 49

tests 26, 89
time out 81
transfer 18
transport 43
textbooks 91

underachiever 67
university 24

workshops 55
writing 95

Preface

Many parents with whom I have come into contact have expressed deep concern about their children's education and have indicated that they would like to play a more meaningful role. However, parents often do not know how to achieve this, especially if they have only a little time at their disposal. Moreover, many parents feel intimidated by schools and are afraid that they may be thought to be interfering when they do take an active interest. This prevents them from becoming involved in assisting both the school and the teachers.

For too long education has been seen as the exclusive domain of schools, and parent participation has therefore been very limited. In recent times, however, there has been a gradual move away from total separation between home and school towards an increasing awareness and recognition of the central role of parents as equal partners in the education process. Education is not solely the responsibility of the teachers. Effective and meaningful education requires the participation and co-operation of both teachers and parents. It is, therefore, accepted that all parents should be actively involved in their children's education. However, to be able to do this, they need information, guidance and support.

The purpose of this guide is to provide parents with basic information on general school matters to enable them to facilitate their children's education and support their children's school. The guide also aims to help parents by increasing their awareness and understanding of their rights and duties with regard to education so that they can make informed decisions about their children's education and ask the right questions. It provides a variety of information on all aspects of the school and suggests practical ways in which parents can become involved in a wide variety of school- and home-based activities without feeling threatened or overburdened. Each chapter deals with a particular topic.

Although this guide is directed in the first instance at parents, it is hoped that teachers, who are also often parents, will find the information just as useful and will use it to enhance their relationship with parents and thus include them in a more meaningful and positive way. In this way, teachers and parents can work together and support each other, thus contributing to the education and well-being of the children, for whose benefit this guide is ultimately intended.

The author
1994

Introduction

For many years there was a clearly-drawn line between home and school, and the roles of parents and teachers were more explicitly defined than they are today. Education was obviously the domain of the school and parents were discouraged from interfering. Parents, therefore, played a very limited role in the school and their children's education. Today the importance of parent involvement in education is widely recognised by teachers, educationists and parents themselves.

What is parent involvement?

Parent involvement can mean many things. Often it is only associated with parents serving on school governing bodies or on parent-teacher associations whose functions are mainly of a fund-raising nature, or helping to organise school activities and events. Parent involvement is much more than merely serving on a school committee. It is the active and willing participation of parents in a wide range of school- and home-based activities. It is manifested in a variety of activities, from supporting and upholding the ethos of the school to supervising children's homework.

In this book the term "parent" is used in its widest meaning to include natural parents, guardians or any other adult who is responsible for a child. Anyone, therefore, who has children in his or her care can and should take an interest in their education. The extent of involvement will depend on various factors. Not all parents have the same interest, time or skills, but no matter what the circumstances may be, every parent can, in some way, help his or her child succeed at school.

Why should parents become more involved in education?

There is wide agreement on the value of parental involvement in children's education. The following reasons for parent involvement are given:
- Parents care about their children's welfare and well-being.
- Parents are the most influential people in their childrens' lives.
- Parents want their children to succeed.
- Parents are primary and natural educators.
- Parents' and teachers' skills complement each other.

- Parents can provide teachers with important information about their children.
- Parents can bring their expertise to the school.
- Parents can influence their children's attitudes towards schooling.
- Parents can motivate children to learn.
- Parents can support discipline and promote good behaviour.
- Parents have certain legal rights regarding their children's education.
- Parents can help with the day-to-day management of the school.
- Parents are responsible by law for their children's education.

How can parents become involved in their children's education and help them succeed at school?

There are many ways in which parents can support the school and so help their children. First of all, it is important to understand how schools work and to have essential information on general school matters. This is dealt with in Part I of this guide. It is also necessary to know how to support and encourage your child at home. This is dealt with in Part II.

Part 1

Know your child's school

You can help your child succeed at school by being better informed about basic school matters. In the first part of this guide, background information, suggestions and practical guidelines on a variety of school matters are presented. Some matters may be dealt with in more detail than others, and some information might be more relevant to you and your child than to others. It should also be borne in mind that education in general, and schools in particular, are undergoing enormous change at present. Schools differ in respect of size, language of instruction, educational goals, facilities, academic performance and so on. Multicultural communities in which the experiences, needs, expectations and aspirations of people differ, are now a reality. Our schools have to cater for these communities.

1. Parental rights and responsibilities in education

Parents as primary educators

Education is primarily the responsibility of parents. Parents are the child's first educators and the most influential people in a child's life. When a child reaches school-going age, the parents transfer part of their responsibility for educating their children to the teacher. In this regard, teachers act on behalf of, and in the place of, parents, while the children are in their care. This does not mean that parents can give up their duty to educate their children. Parents should continue to play a major role in their children's education.

Duties and responsibilities

The main responsibilities of parents are to care for their children and meet their obligation to send them to school. Parents have a duty to support their children, which means providing for their physical, material and emotional needs, and to protect them.

Compulsory education

Schooling is compulsory and therefore it is the parents' duty to make sure that their children attend school on a regular basis. Legal steps can be taken against parents, guardians and others who do not comply with this law. Exemption from compulsory school attendance may be granted under certain conditions, however, such as serious ill health.

Parental choice

Parents can exercise a certain amount of choice regarding the type of school they wish their children to attend. Parental choice may, however, be limited by factors such as financial constraints, school admission policies and locality. For example, parents wishing to send their children to a particular school may be prevented from doing so because they do not live within the feeder area, that is, the particular area directly served by the school. Preference is given to children living within the school's feeder area, but this should not discourage you from applying to a school outside your immediate community if this is the school of your choice.

Right to information

Parents have a right to be informed of their children's performance, progress and behaviour. Parents should, therefore, have the opportunity to meet teachers and receive school reports regularly, and to have access to information affecting their children. Parents also have the right to be informed about any matter relating to their child's education. In certain cases, however, the school may refuse to provide information concerning a child if it is not in the child's best interest. IQ scores are an example.

Parents and the curriculum

Although parents do not have any official say over the content of the general curriculum and the way in which it is taught, they do have certain rights concerning some aspects of the curriculum, such as religious and sex education. This issue is dealt with in Chapter 4. Parents do, however, also have the right to discuss curricular matters with their children's teachers so that they understand what is being taught, and to be informed of any changes that may take place with regard to content and particular teaching methods.

2. How schools work

Schools are complex organisations. To become effectively involved in your child's education, it is important that you understand the different positions, roles, tasks and responsibilities of the school staff and how the school functions.

Schools are normally organised as hierarchies, with the principal at the top of the pyramid and pupils at the bottom. The following organisational diagrams show the different levels of authority and division of work in two schools of different size.

A medium-sized primary school may be structured in the following way:

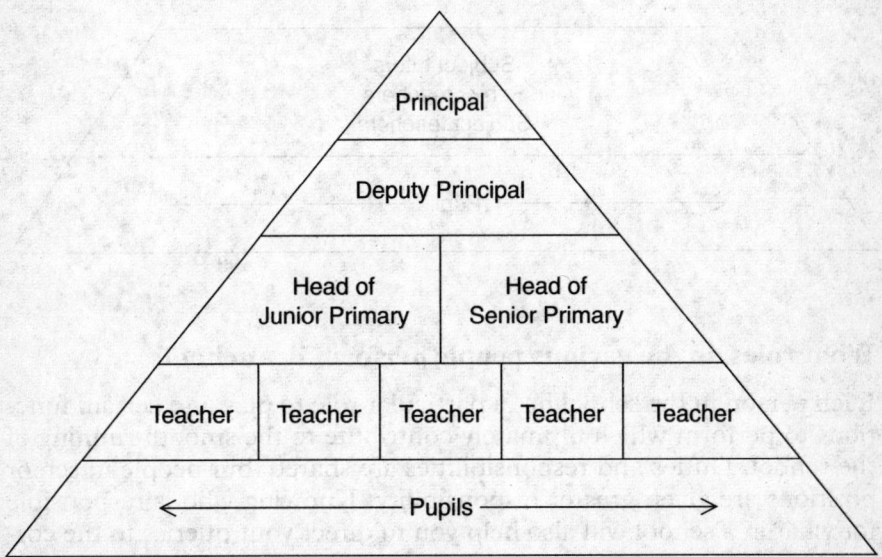

A large secondary school might be structured in this way:

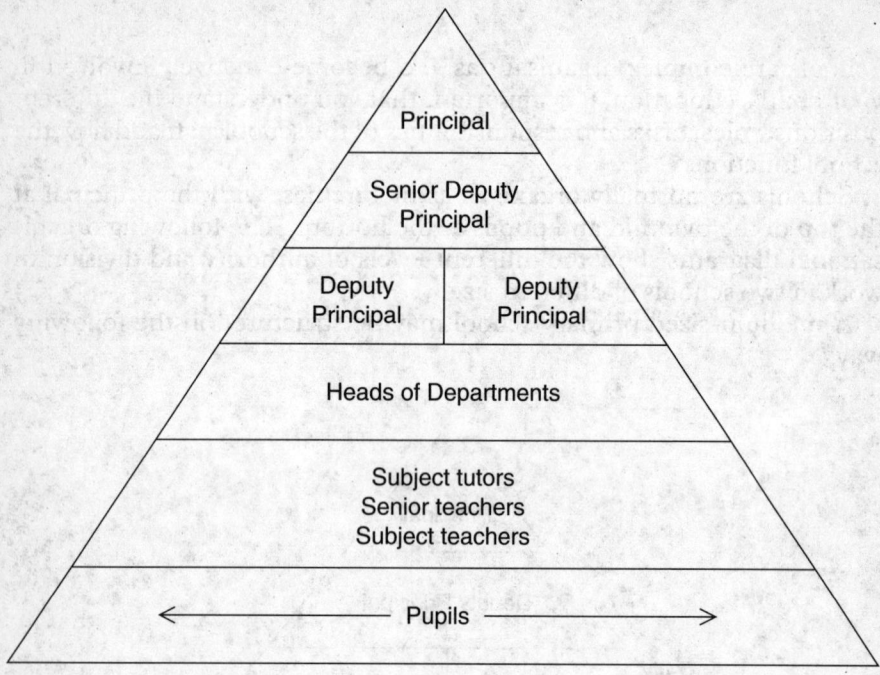

What roles do the various people perform in a school?

Each person in the school has a particular role to play and certain functions to perform which ultimately contribute to the smooth running of the school. Duties and responsibilities are shared, but people in senior positions are given greater responsibility. Knowing who is responsible for what in a school will also help you to direct your queries to the correct person.

Principals
Principals fulfil the key role in schools. They are the professional leaders and managers of a school and are responsible for managing all areas within a school.

The general tasks of a principal include:
• teaching;

6

- developing the school policy;
- planning and implementing the school curriculum;
- organising the school timetable;
- reports and correspondence;
- bookkeeping;
- acquisition of stock;
- liaising with education authorities;
- liaising with parents and the community;
- drawing up the school budget;
- collecting and administering school funds;
- school discipline;
- staff development;
- tests and examinations;
- the extracurricular programme;
- managing school hostels; and
- marketing the school.

As you can see, a principal has many tasks. Some of these are delegated to senior staff, although the principal is ultimately responsible for all school matters.

Senior deputy principals/deputy principals
Deputy principals work very closely with the principal. When a principal is absent the deputy principal assumes responsibility for school administration. The deputy principal serves as the link between the principal and staff.

A deputy principal's normal functions include:
- assisting with the drawing up of the school policy;
- planning the school timetable;
- drawing up duty rosters for staff;
- controlling the syllabuses;
- guiding pupils in their choice of subjects;
- organising school functions;
- supervising the school prefects and/or students' representative council;
- assisting with the school budget;
- providing guidance in subject meetings;
- staff evaluation;
- administering textbooks and equipment; and
- maintaining discipline and administering punishment.

Heads of Departments

Heads of Departments (HODs) are middle managers in the school. They are responsible for the organisation and administration of a particular department. Departments may be classified according to a particular age group, such as the junior primary department, according to a subject, such as mathematics, or a field of subjects, such as the humanities.

General responsibilities of heads of departments include:
- ensuring that the education programme runs smoothly;
- estimating the budget for the department;
- controlling internal tests and examinations;
- supporting and guiding teachers in their departments;
- giving advice on teaching methods;
- moderating schemes of work;
- evaluating pupils;
- evaluating teachers;
- control of books; and
- moderating examination papers.

Standard tutors

Standard tutors are responsible for taking care of pupils in a particular standard. They monitor the pupils' work and progress, and give them guidance on matters of general educational concern.

Subject tutors

Subject tutors are usually senior teachers who are in charge of a particular subject. They provide expert advice on the development and teaching of a particular subject. Subject tutors are responsible for organising subject meetings. They also give advice on subject policy, subject aims and subject evaluation.

Teachers

Teachers can be either class or subject teachers. A class teacher, such as a Sub A teacher or Standard 2 teacher, stays with one class and is responsible for teaching that class all subjects except for a few, such as music and physical education, which are taught by specialist teachers. A subject teacher, on the other hand, may teach one or more subjects, such as English and History, to different classes and different standards.

The professional responsibilities of teachers include:
- drawing up the class timetable;
- planning the contents of lessons;
- classroom management
- evaluating pupils' work;
- writing pupils' reports;
- liaising with parents;
- attending subject meetings;
- maintaining classroom discipline;
- assisting with extracurricular activities;
- keeping a class register;
- keeping a record of all his or her pupils' work;
- controlling stock.

Non-teaching staff
Non-teaching staff, such as secretaries, typists, laboratory technicians and maintenance staff, play an equally important role in the school. Parents will come into regular contact with secretaries and it is, therefore, important to know who they are, their names and their particular role, so that you are able to direct queries to the correct person.

School governing bodies
Most schools have a governing body or management council. The school governing body is a formal statutory committee consisting of the principal and parents elected from the parent community. The governing body represents the parents and assists the principal with the day-to-day management of the school.

Important school data

Knowing how a school works will go a long way in helping you to understand and appreciate the roles and responsibilities of different members of staff. There is also some basic information about the school which you should obtain at the beginning of each school year which can be displayed in a suitable place for easy reference. You can make use of the reproducible page on page 102.

Do you know the .....
- name of the principal?
- name of the deputy principal?
- school address?

- school telephone number?
- name of the secretary/receptionist?
- name of the standard tutor?
- school hours?
- name of the chairman of the school governing body?
- dates of the school holidays?

3. Choosing the right school

Choosing the right school for your child is very important. Today parents have greater freedom of choice, and it is worthwhile to look around for a school that is the most suitable for your child. Certain factors, such as the distance of the school from your home, entrance examinations, school fees and availability of space, could limit your choice, however.

Types of schools

Education departments make provision for various types of pre-primary, primary and secondary schools, catering for a wide variety of needs and interests.

- **Pre-primary schools** provide informal education for 3- to 6-year-olds. These schools are generally run by churches, welfare organisations and private agencies. Pre-primary schools are required by law to register with an education department. However, pre-primary education is not compulsory and is usually not free. It does, however, play a very important role in preparing children for primary school. Children who have attended pre-primary schools have a distinct advantage over other children.
- **Primary schools** provide formal education for 7- to 13-year-olds. Education is general and informative. The fundamental aim of primary education is to master the basic principles of language, reading, writing and arithmetic. There is no choice of subjects.
- **Secondary schools** provide formal education for 14- to 18-year-olds. At the secondary level there is a choice of subjects and more differentiation takes place.
- **Special schools** have been established to provide education for pupils with special needs. There are schools for the physically handicapped, the cerebral palsied, the deaf and the blind. These schools are often run by church groups, welfare organisations or private agencies.
- **Community schools** are established and controlled by the community. They offer a wide variety of courses for young people and adults.

At the present time (1994), schools can be classified into three broad groups, private, state and state-aided schools. The difference between these categories lies mainly in the locus of control and the financing of the schools.

11

- **Private schools** are run by private individuals and groups, and church organisations. Private schools offer a high standard of education. School fees are compulsory and relatively high. Private schools can apply for a state subsidy but many do not, since they prefer to retain their autonomy. Private schools must be registered with an education department.
- **State schools** are managed and controlled by the state. The state pays all costs. School fees are not compulsory at state schools, but parents are expected to make a financial contribution to the school funds to maintain facilities and purchase equipment.
- **State-aided schools** are managed by the principal and school governing body on behalf of the parent community. The parent community is responsible for financing the school, but teachers' salaries are paid by the state. School fees are therefore compulsory in state-aided schools.

Within each category, there are a number of schools that cater for specialist needs. For example, there are schools for the handicapped, schools for children with learning problems, and art, ballet and music schools. Some schools cater for particular fields of study, and include agricultural, commercial and technical schools.

Multicultural schools

Schools are undergoing fundamental change at present and it is important for parents to keep up to date with developments in education, especially in terms of school management and organisation, school enrolment, school finances and the curriculum.

One of the most significant changes that has taken place recently is the opening of previously segregated schools to children of all racial groups. This move has been welcomed by many principals, teachers, parents and pupils, and is seen as a major step towards creating a nonracial education system. The change has, however, generated a great deal of fear and anxiety because of the wide range of new demands and challenges it places on schools and all those involved.

Principals and teachers are now required to meet the needs of children from diverse cultural, linguistic, socio-economic and educational backgrounds. This increasing diversity in school populations has resulted in the need for schools to keep up with the changing circumstances, while at the same time maintaining their existing standards (Lemmer & Squelch 1993). This means that principals and teachers need to reexamine and re-evaluate existing school policies and practices to determine to what extent they meet the needs and expectations of all children and parents, and decide what changes should take place. Merely opening the school doors to children of all cultural groups does not guarantee that newcomers will benefit from equal educational opportunities. The *status quo* must be adapted to suit the different needs of individuals.

To this end, many educationists advocate the need for multicultural education. In a nutshell, it means adapting the entire school system to create suitable learning environments for culturally diverse groups of pupils. Multicultural education is an important approach to the education of culturally diverse groups of children because it acknowledges the equal rights of all cultural groups in a society, advocates equal educational opportunities, emphasises a high standard of education and is synonymous with good teaching. It is also important because it aims to develop positive attitudes towards all groups, to reduce racial and cultural prejudice and to prepare children for meaningful participation in a multicultural society. Implementing multicultural education, therefore, means that aspects such as the school policy, curriculum, teaching methods, instructional materials (books, worksheets, pictures, etc.), communication, language teaching, pupil evaluation, the school counselling programme and the composition of the school staff need to reflect the multicultural nature of society.

The success of multicultural education depends on the co-operation of teachers, parents and pupils. Parents have a very important role to play in helping and supporting schools to meet these new demands and challenges. Parents are a valuable source of information and can help principals and teachers understand their needs, concerns and expectations. School governing bodies should be fully informed about the needs of the school in terms of staff development, resources such as books and other instructional materials, and educational support programmes, especially language and bridging programmes.

In a multicultural class children have to interact with other children from backgrounds different to their own. Parents have a crucial role to play in preparing their children for interaction with other children. They need to set an example and teach their children to value, appreciate and respect other people. Children need to learn the value of cultural diversity, to be knowledgeable about other cultural groups and to see themselves and others as individuals, differing in many ways, yet essentially similar.

How to find out about schools

It is not usually difficult to obtain important information about a school. There are many sources where this can be obtained.

School boards

Most regions have a school board. School boards are local education authorities which are largely responsible for managing and supervising educational facilities within a district. They are listed in the telephone directory and can provide useful information on schools and educational facilities in your area.

School prospectus

Many schools publish their own prospectuses which are obtainable directly from the school. A prospectus is usually in the form of a brochure or booklet providing details on various aspects, often including a history of the school.

Parents

It is a good idea to talk to parents whose children attend the school you have in mind for your child. They can provide valuable information about the school. It is, however, very important to use your discretion when assessing this information.

Visits to schools

It is always advisable to visit a school before enrolling your child. Draw up a list of potential schools in order of priority, and then visit as many as possible so that you can obtain first-hand information about each one. Remember that it is important to make an appointment beforehand.

Appointments can be requested in writing or telephonically. Ask to view the school's facilities. Before visiting the school, think about what you want to know and write down a few questions you would like to ask. This will ensure that you do not forget to ask pertinent questions.

Open days

Many schools arrange open days for parents of prospective pupils. These are often advertised in the local press. Make use of these opportunities to visit the school and view its facilities, to meet and talk to teachers and to meet other parents.

Guidelines on choosing a school

Many factors will influence your choice of school. When choosing a school remember that you and your child must be satisfied with what it has to offer. You have a right to know about matters such as the qualifications of teachers, the school's academic achievements, its educational goals and its values.

The answers to the following questions can help you evaluate and select a school.

- Is the school conveniently situated?
- What public transport is available?
- Are school fees compulsory and how much are they?
- What is the school's enrolment (the number of pupils)?
- What is the ratio of pupils to teachers?
- Is the school co-educational?
- Is the school multiracial?
- Does the school offer the subjects your child requires?
- Are the academic standards of the school satisfactory?
- Is the school staffed by well-qualified teachers?
- What is the language medium of instruction? Will your child be able to cope with the language required?
- Does the school offer academic support programmes?
- Does the school have adequate academic and non-academic facilities?
- Does the extracurricular programme include activities in which your child is interested?
- Does the school have a students' representative council?
- What is the school's policy on religious education?
- Does the school subscribe to or encourage a specific religion? If so, what provision is made for children of other religions?
- Is the discipline of the school satisfactory? Is there a clearly stated code of conduct?
- Does the school provide after-school care? Are there study centres?
- Does the school have hostel (boarding) facilities?
- Do the values and ethos of the school fit in with your own system of values?

You can make use of the reproducible page on page 101 of this guide.

Making the final choice

Select a few schools. Make a list of the most important features of each one. Compare the schools and then make your final choice. Remember that your child may not automatically be accepted by that school, so you should have alternatives. If your child is starting primary or high school, it is advisable to select and apply to a school well in advance, and put his or her name on the waiting list.

Name of school	Plus points	Minus points
1.		
2.		
3.		
4.		

Involving your child

Involve your child when choosing a school. Discuss the matter openly and frankly with him or her. Find out what he or she feels is important and which school or schools he or she would prefer to attend, as well as the reasons for his or her choice. Take these views into consideration when you make the final choice.

Preparing for an interview

When you enrol your child the school will expect both you and your child to attend an interview. Interviews are essential for gathering information about the prospective pupil and his or her family. It is important for both of you to ask questions about the school in order to determine its suitability. The interview should be a two-way communication so that each party can obtain all the necessary and relevant information. Asking questions also shows that you are interested in the school and know what you want.

Asking the right questions
Often parents and the child are not sure what questions they should ask at such an interview. It is only afterwards that relevant questions come to mind. As a result, the parents do not obtain all the information they need and they leave feeling dissatisfied.

The following is a list of possible questions that could be asked. Write down these and others, so that you are well prepared for the interview and know beforehand what you are going to ask. Feel free to make notes during the interview for later reference.
• What does the school expect from us, the parents?
• What subjects does the school offer?
• How many pupils are there in the school?
• What is the pupil/teacher ratio?
• What are the promotion requirements?
• What academic support is provided for pupils with special learning needs?
• Can we visit the class/subject teacher at times other than on parent evenings? How do we go about arranging this?
• In what extracurricular activities will our child be expected to take part?
• What is the school's policy on homework?
• What are the requirements in regard to a school uniform?
• Does the school stream pupils according to their ability?

Important information and documents
Always be well prepared for an interview. Information the school may require from you could include:
• a history of the family;
• personal details of parents
• personal details of the child;
• details of the child's school career;
• the child's academic record;
• the child's interests;
• reasons for choosing the school;
• expectations of the family; and
• medical information.

On enrolment, parents are required to complete an enrolment form. To avoid any problems or delays, it would help to have the following documents on hand:

- birth certificate of the child;
- identification documents;
- previous report/s;
- testimonials/reference letter/s; and
- immunisation certificate.

School contracts

Many schools now require parents to sign a legal contract. This is a fairly recent development. These contracts are generally concerned with ensuring that parents fulfil their obligations with regard to payment of school fees. Many contracts contain indemnity clauses which have been a point of dispute between some parents and schools. Make sure that you fully understand the wording and contents of the contract, and the implications it holds for you. If you are still uncertain about signing the contract, contact the education department concerned and obtain clarity from them on any problem you may have. It is also advisable to discuss the contract with a legal expert before signing. The issue of indemnities is dealt with further in Chapter 8.

Changing schools

From time to time circumstances make it necessary for children to change schools. Sometimes the family has to move to a new area or the parents are not satisfied with the school, or perhaps the school does not offer the required subjects. It is, however, not advisable to move children too often or for reasons that are not absolutely necessary. Changing schools is disruptive and can be traumatic for the child. For this reason it is also not advisable to move children at crucial stages, such as Standards 4 and 5 or Standards 9 and 10.

If you do choose to move your child to another school, the principal must be advised in writing well in advance. The principal will then furnish you with an official transfer certificate which must be given to the principal of the new school. A principal may not refuse to provide such a certificate if it has been requested by the parents.

Choosing a pre-school

At a pre-school, children between the ages of 3 and 6 receive formative education in an informal, but structured way. Pre-school education is valuable in that it prepares the child for primary school, and facilitates the transition from home to school. Unlike day-care centres, which are usually not necessarily staffed by qualified people, a pre-school has to have some fully qualified pre-school teachers on its staff.

Although it is not compulsory, parents are encouraged to send their children to pre-school because it can play such an important role in the child's intellectual, social and moral development.

The pre-school curriculum focuses on developing a variety of basic social and intellectual skills, such as the following:
- **Musical development**: learning songs, listening to music, learning rhythm and movement;
- **Language development**: extending vocabulary and speech;
- **Listening skills**: following directions and instructions;
- Developing **social skills**: learning to work with others, sharing, developing self-control, learning rules, learning to co-operate, learning to resolve conflict;
- Developing **creativity**;
- Developing **numerical skills**: learning to count, sequencing, matching, ordering, sharing and measurement;
- **Physical development**: learning to balance, catch, throw, skip and jump;
- **Aesthetic development**: children are exposed to, and encouraged to experiment with, a variety of art and craft materials.

Pre-schools should be fun, interesting and exciting places in which to learn and grow. Choosing a suitable pre-school is just as important as selecting a primary school.

The following questions will help you to choose a pre-school:
- Are the staff qualified?
- Is the school conveniently situated?
- Is there sufficient space for children to play and run around?
- Is there adequate play and learning equipment?
- Are the rooms bright, cheerful, and well ventilated?
- Is the environment safe and secure?
- Are there adequate toilet facilities?
- How many children attend?
- Is there adequate supervision?
- Are the staff trained in first aid?
- Do the children look happy?
- Is the school organised without being too structured and rigid?
- What play materials are provided for the children?
- Are there sufficient books for children to read or look at?
- Is there a suitable place where children can rest or sleep?

4. The school curriculum

Generally, schools are not keen to involve parents in matters concerning the curriculum. However, understanding what the curriculum is and how it is arranged, is one way of supporting your child. Knowing what has to be studied will also make it possible for you to help your child plan his or her work.

The school curriculum is the programme of work followed by a school and is drawn up by specialists in the education departments. The general curriculum is designed around subject areas or fields of study. At present all the education departments follow a core curriculum, which has provincial and regional variations. The curriculum is currently undergoing change in preparation for a new, single, non-racial education department.

The primary school curriculum

The primary school curriculum focuses on providing a general, formative education. The emphasis is on reading, writing, language and arithmetic skills. The children are also required to study history, geography, general science, health and media education. Non-examination subjects such as religious education, art, guidance, music and physical education, form a compulsory part of the curriculum.

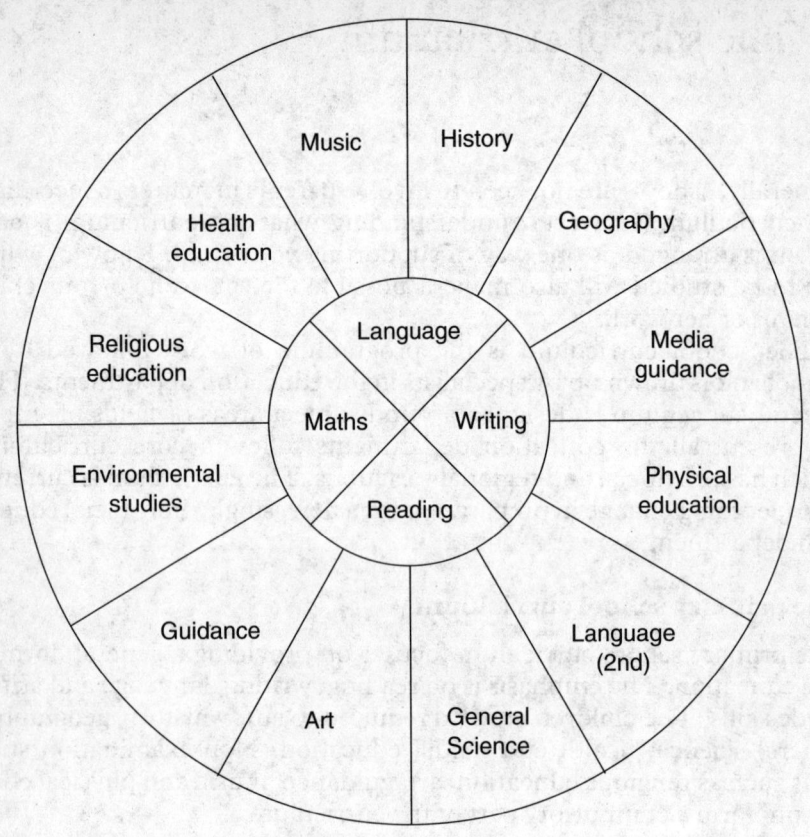

4.2 The secondary school curriculum

The junior secondary phase includes Standards 6 and 7. During this phase pupils study basically the same subjects as in the primary school, and there is little choice. Pupils take up to 13 subjects during the first two years of high school. Some schools focus on different areas of the curriculum. For example, one school may offer several languages while another will offer more commercial or technical subjects. It is important to find out exactly what subjects are offered at a school before enrolling your child.

The senior secondary phase, which includes Standards 8, 9 and 10, allows for differences of subject choice and teaching levels. Pupils can choose subjects from the different fields of study at different levels, namely higher, standard or lower grade.

Subjects are arranged in the following fields of study:

Natural Sciences	Languages	Practical studies	Humanities	Commercial
Physics	English	Home Economics	History	Business
Chemistry	Afrikaans	Industrial Arts	Geography	Economics
Biology	Zulu	Art	Religious Ed.	Accountancy
Maths	Sotho	Music	etc.	Typing
etc.	Other	etc.		etc.

Subject levels

Subjects can be taken at higher, standard or lower grade. Subjects on the higher grade are taught at an advanced level and tend to include some theory.

Subjects taught on the standard grade focus more on content and are thus accessible to most pupils. The content of lower grade subjects is relatively simple and more practically-orientated. Children who experience difficulty with learning may take subjects on the lower grade.

Making the right subject choice

Towards the end of Standard 7 pupils select a set of six subjects, apart from the compulsory non-examination subjects, which they will study for the last three years of secondary school. In certain cases pupils can choose more than six subjects. Choosing subjects at this age can be difficult, because very few children have actually decided on a career path. Children often simply choose the same subjects as their friends or they choose because they like the teacher or because the subjects are seemingly easy.

You can help your child make a correct decision by finding out more about the requirements for different careers, university and college entrance requirements, and the nature of the school subject. Talk to the subject teachers and the school guidance teacher to obtain sound advice. When you help your child choose subjects it is important to consider his or her ability, interests, current grades and performance, and possible career options. It is usually safest to choose a set of subjects that will keep most doors open. Subject choice can be limited by school facilities, the availability of qualified teachers, the number of pupils wanting to take the subject and examination requirements.

University entrance

In order for children to obtain a university entrance matric, at least four subjects chosen from the required groups of subjects must be taken on higher grade. One of the subjects must be a first language. It is very important to obtain information on the groups of subjects from the school before your child makes his or her final choice in Standard 7. Schools may offer different subject options, depending on the facilities available. For example, not all schools offer computer studies or technika (electronics).

The following are a few examples of subject options for entrance to a university, provided that four of the subjects are taken on the higher grade.

Option A	Option B	Option C	Option D
English	English	English	English
Afrikaans	Zulu	Afrikaans	N. Sotho
Maths	Maths	Maths	Science
Science	Science	Biology	Maths
Geography	Biology	Home Economics	Biology
Biology	History	Art	Computer studies

Do parents have a say over curriculum content?

Parents have no say over the content of subjects or how they are taught. One of the main reasons for this is that it is believed that the curriculum must be left to the professionals and that parents may not interfere in the professional side of the school. Parents should, however, be fully aware of what the curriculum contains as far as it concerns their children. There are also a few areas of the curriculum in which parents do have some say. These are concerned with religious, sex and physical education.

Religious education

Religious education is a compulsory part of the school curriculum. However, the law provides for the religious convictions of parents to be considered. Parents who do not wish their children to attend religious education classes or acts of worship may request that their children be exempted. The request must be made in writing by a parent.

Sex education
Sex education is not yet a part of the formal curriculum. Here the discretion lies with the principal and parents. Parents have a right to know the content of any sex education programme and by whom it is to be taught. Schools that discuss their policy on sex education with parents have less difficulty in obtaining parental approval.

Physical education
Physical education is also a compulsory part of the formal curriculum. Physical education should be taught by specialist teachers who are fully responsible for the safety of pupils during the physical education class. However, no pupil may participate in physical education if this could be detrimental to him or her, or if the child has a particular medical condition that prevents participation.

Parents can help their children and the school by providing both the school and physical education teachers with essential medical information. If your child cannot participate in physical education for medical reasons, inform the school in writing and provide the relevant medical certificates. If your child is suffering from a temporary illness, it is also essential to send a note to the teacher concerned requesting permission for him or her to be excused for that period.

An essential requirement for physical education is to have the appropriate dress. Ensure that you know on which days your child has physical education and that he or she has the correct clothes. The clothes should also be clearly labelled with the child's name. School insurance does not cover loss of possessions.

5. Examinations

Examinations form a necessary part of the school programme. They are a means of evaluating a child's achievements and progress, and determining whether or not learning objectives have been attained. Promotion from one standard to the next depends largely on how well a child performs in internal tests and examinations. Internal examinations are compiled by teachers and are written two or three times a year. Class tests are written throughout the year.

Promotion requirements

The end-of-the-year promotion mark is usually made up of class assignments, class tests and examination marks. The way in which the final mark is calculated may vary from school to school. It is important to find out the promotion requirements for your child's school.

Promotion requirements might look like this:

Grade 1 to Standard 2
1. A minimum of 50% overall

Standards 3 to 5
1. An aggregate of 40%
2. A minimum of 40% in English
3. A minimum of 34% in all other subjects

or

Standards 2 to 5
1. English D
2. Afrikaans E

3. Mathematics E
4. Culturals F

Standards 8 and 9
1. An aggregate of 40%
2. A minimum of 40% for HG (higher grade) subjects
3. A minimum of $33\frac{1}{3}\%$ for SG (standard grade) subjects

Standards 6 and 7
1. 40% for 1st language
2. A minimum of 35% for all other subjects
3. If three subjects are failed, the child is not promoted

External examinations

At the end of Standard 10, that is, the final year of schooling, pupils write external examinations. These examinations are set and marked by an external examinations committee. Before the pupils write these final (matric) examinations, they write a set of preliminary examinations. These preliminary examinations are set internally and provide pupils with an opportunity to practise for the final examinations.

Promotion requirements for matric examinations

To obtain a university exemption certificate, pupils need to take at least six subjects, four of which should be on the higher grade. A pass mark for a higher grade subject is 40% and for a standard grade subject $33\frac{1}{3}$%. At least five subjects must be passed to obtain a matric certificate. A five-subject matric will not provide entrance to a university.

Under certain circumstances a higher grade subject can be converted to a standard grade subject. For example: HG – $33\frac{1}{3}$% (F) – fail, can be converted to SG – $33\frac{1}{3}$% (E) – pass (HG = higher grade, SG = standard grade). Note that only the symbol and not the mark changes.

Remember that even if a pupil obtains a university exemption certificate it does not mean he or she will automatically be accepted for a tertiary course. Universities and colleges have different requirements for courses so it is important to establish beforehand what these requirements are.

Re-taking external examinations

Often pupils do badly in the final examination, thereby jeopardising their chances of further education. If they fail an examination or obtain very low marks at the end of Standard 10, they do have the opportunity to rewrite the examination. These are called supplementary examinations and are usually written in January/February. Pupils who fail more than a stipulated number of examinations, or fail overall, are usually required to repeat the school year. Consult the school on how to go about rewriting an examination. Note that additional examination fees are payable.

What are examination fees?

There has recently been strong resistance to paying examination fees. Up to now, matriculation pupils were required to pay an examination fee to offset the costs of the production and administration of the examination papers, that is, the setting, printing, distribution, marking and moderation of examination papers. This fee could be implemented again in the future.

Tips to help your child prepare for examinations

Examination time is a stressful period for many children. Tension and anxiety can have a negative affect on your child's performance. By helping him or her prepare for examinations you can help reduce the level of stress and anxiety he or she may experience. Pay particular attention to the following:

- allocate a quiet place for your child to study;
- encourage your child to study at a regular time each day;
- help your child plan his or her time. Divide up the work so that sufficient time is allocated to each subject;
- display the examination timetable in a prominent and visible place;
- make sure your child eats healthy, balanced meals. Children love to eat snacks while they study, so provide them with healthy snacks such as fruit, nuts and health bars;
- make sure they get plenty of rest as well as exercise;
- monitor and reduce television viewing time; and
- do not allow your child to take any form of medication to improve alertness. On the other hand, if your child has difficulty sleeping and is very anxious, consult your doctor or local health clinic for advice.

Chapter 19 contains further hints on how to help your child study.

6. Records and reports

Throughout a child's school life important information about him or her is recorded and filed. This information is accumulative and goes with the child from one standard to the next, and from one school to another. The information recorded in pupils' files is generally grouped into the following categories:
- Personal particulars
- Family details
- Academic progress
- School achievements
- Medical records
- General behaviour
- References.

It is important to ensure that the information given to a school is accurate, up-to-date and complete: for example, change of address, change in family structure, medical certificates and so on. It is also important to keep your own record at home of important reports, documents and letters.

Right to information

Parents have a right to be informed about their child's progress and behaviour, and any other matter that concerns their child's welfare and education. Not all information is accessible to parents, however, especially if it is deemed not to be in the best interests of the child. In general, parents are not permitted to see pupils' personal files containing confidential information valuable to teachers but not necessary for parents, especially if it could cause unnecessary stress.

IQ (intelligence quotient) scores are a case in point. Parents are generally not permitted to know their child's IQ score. This is mainly because IQ scores are not always a true reflection of a child's ability and can be very misleading. Information on IQ scores can also lead to unnecessary stress and concern on the one hand or unrealistic expectations on the other. Categorising a child on the basis of a single IQ score can be detrimental to him or her. The use of IQ scores as a means of measuring a child's intelligence and predicting performance is highly questionable.

Teachers often record confidential comments and observations in a child's file. It is therefore important to maintain regular contact with teachers and to keep track of your child's progress and behaviour. Parents can ask that certain information not be placed on record if it is not of great importance but could have a negative influence on a child later on in his or her school career. Teachers cannot be sued for libel by parents or pupils for writing negative comments about a child unless it can be proved that it was done so maliciously and unfairly – which seldom is the case.

Right to confidentiality

Schools have important and often highly sensitive information about children on record and therefore have an obligation to ensure the confidentiality of this information. This is not a simple issue because at times it is necessary for principals or teachers to use the information in a way that might be in breach of this confidentiality. Decisions on the use of the information should not be taken lightly, and it should only be used when it is in the very best interests of the child.

Accumulative records

Details of pupils' tests, examinations and other scholastic achievements are recorded on accumulative record cards. These records are kept up to date so that the information can be used by teachers. The information they contain is not made available to parents, but principals and teachers should keep you posted with regard to your child's progress and any problems that might be reflected on the record card.

School reports

Pupils are issued with a school report at regular intervals, such as at the end of each quarter or term. Reports indicate the child's name and standard, the number of children in the class, the position in the class achieved by the child, a list of the subjects taken and the marks obtained for each subject, the class average for each subject, general remarks by the teacher and an indication of whether the child has passed or failed. The report is signed by the teacher and principal, and must also be signed by the parent.

Unfortunately, few reports are designed to provide space for parents' comments on the content of the report or for any additional information the parent might require. If your child's report does not provide space for comments or queries, you should still follow up the report with the teacher(s) concerned.

Reports generally give a good indication of a child's's progress, achievements, standard of work and conduct. The information is usually expressed as symbols or percentages, for example C or 67%. In the junior primary phase, pupils' work is graded according to a scale of 1 – 5, with 1 being the highest and 5 the lowest. Grades expressed as symbols and percentages do not necessarily tell one much, and are therefore supplemented by brief comments written by the teachers.

Parents, however, often complain that the comments are not always helpful because they are too general or vague, or because they are stated in difficult technical language. For example, comments such as "can work harder", "great improvement – but occasional relapses" and "diction is average" require some explanation. You need to know exactly what the situation is and how it can be dealt with both at school and at home. Comments can also be confusing if they do not appear to match the mark. For example, Peter obtains 50% for geography and the comment is that he "is working well"! It is therefore a good idea to use parents' evenings to ask the teacher to explain the report and the comments. If the report is very poor do not wait a term before discussing it with the teacher(s) – make an appointment to talk about it immediately.

Find out from the teacher(s) what the reasons are for the poor marks, but most important of all, establish what can be done to help your child improve his or her marks. The best results are achieved when teachers, parents and pupils work together – this applies whether the pupil is in Standard 2 or Standard 9.

Case study
Let's consider the following situation:

Sam Davis is in Sandard 8. He is a confident, well-adjusted boy. He seems to do his homework and his teacher never complains about his work or behaviour. At a parents' evening Mrs Davis is told that her son is doing fine. At the end of the second term Mrs Davis receives her son's report and to her dismay learns that Sam's grades have dropped dramatically and that he is at risk of failing the year unless "he tries harder".

Mrs Davis discusses the report with her son. At the beginning of the third term, she attends another parents' meeting and is told that her "son is doing fine but he needs to work a little harder". She leaves the meeting most disturbed because she still does not understand why Sam is doing so badly and is worried that he might fail at the end of the third term unless something is done.

What do you do in a situation like this?
In a situation like this, it is very important to find out exactly what the nature of the problem is and decide on ways to help your child. It is not sufficient for the teacher to merely say that "he must work harder", nor should you expect the teacher to deal with the matter on his or her own. Both the teacher and the parent should be willing to discuss the problem and come up with a solution in order to ensure that the child succeeds. This can be achieved by following this procedure:

* Identify problems and weaknesses in the child's work and/or behaviour;
* Identify possible reasons for the problem. For example, too much sport, too little time spent on homework, ill-health, being distracted by friends, inadequate supervision, failure to understand the work, or the child has fallen behind and can't keep up;
* Decide on ways in which you and the teacher can help. For example, the teacher might agree to spend some extra time explaining the work and checking to see that the child understands the work, and that he or she is keeping up.
  The teacher can also monitor the child's work more closely and keep the parents informed. The parents, on the other hand, could agree to supervise homework, help organise a study programme or arrange for extra tuition.
* The most important step in this process is to discuss the problem and the solutions with the child, and seek his or her support and co-oper-ation. Allow the child to participate in decisions about his or her work.

Examples of reports
On pages 33 and 34 are examples of two reports. The first one is straight-forward, the second one more complicated.

A simple report form

Name of pupil ...PETER TODD... Number of pupils in the class ...34...

Standard ....8............ Position in class ....17...........

Date ...28 March 1944...

Subject	Marks obtained	Symbol	Class average
English	68	C	D
Afrikaans	54	D	D
Zulu	61	C	C
Mathematics	32	F	D
Science	76	B	D
History	58	D	C

Average Percentage ...58%... Pass/~~Fail~~

Remarks ...Good work! Keep it up.
Try harder at Mathematics...

Conduct ...Good...

Teacher ...A. B. Mann...

Principal ...(Mrs) A. Louw... Parent ....

A more complicated type of report

SUBJECT	25	100	STD-AV.
English T1		63 C	65
English T2		66 C	69
English T3		63 C	64
Afrikaans T1		65 C	62
Afrikaans T2		57 D	61
Afrikaans T3		61 C	60
Mathematics T1		68 C	73
Mathematics T2		76 B	74
Mathematics T3		52 D	67
History T1	14	D	18
History T2	15	C	17
History T3	17	C	17
Geography T1	18	B	16
Geography T2	18	B	16
Geography T2	17	C	16
Science T1	15	C	18
Science T2	20	A	19
Science T3	10	E	19
Health T1	21	A	19
Health T2	17	C	18
Health T3	20	A	18
Sub-Total T1		68 C	71
Sub-Total T2		70 B	70
Sub-Total T3		73 B	70
Total (%) T1		66 C	68
Total (%) T2		67 C	68
Total (%) T3		62 C	65

**PROMOTION REQUIREMENTS –
Std 2, 3 and 4**
English D
Mathematics E and Culturals F or
Mathematics F and Culturals E

Value of Symbols		**Examination to Year Mark Ratio**
A +	90% to 100%	
A	80% to 89%	Std 2 –
B	70% to 79%	Exam. 20% Year 80%
C	60% to 69%	Std 3 –
D	50% to 59%	Exam. 30% Year 70%
E	40% to 49%	Std 4 –
F	35% to 39%	Exam. 40% Year 60%
G	30% to 34%	Std 5 –
H	Below 30%	Exam. 50% Year 50%

Religious Instruction	A
Bantu Language	
Physical Education	B
Days Absent	0

Remarks *Gillian's work is satisfactory but she is working below her potential in Science*

Term Commences	
CLASS TEACHER	*Steve Brown*
HEADMASTER	*G. M. Smith*
SIGNATURE OF PARENT	

What questions could you ask about the second report?

The second report gives very few comments and the mark system looks quite complicated. When you discuss such a report with a teacher you essentially want to determine how well your child is doing and if he or she is experiencing any difficulty with the level of work being done. This is how you go about it:

- obtain clarification on what the different symbols mean;
- establish what the comment "is working below potential" means;
- find out how the term mark is calculated and what percentage of the term mark counts towards the final mark; and
- establish the reason for the drop in the science mark and what can be done to improve it.

Teacher-parent-pupil contracts

One way of ensuring that there will be an improvement in the child's work is to sign a form of contract. A contract is merely a way of recording what has been decided. It describes what work is to be completed and gives the completion date. The following are examples of appropriate contracts. You can also make use of the reproducible page on page 105 of this guide.

Example 1:

I need to improve my maths grades.

My plan is to ...

1. ....

2. ....

3. ....

I will complete this work by ....

Signed

Pupil ....

Parent ....

Teacher ....

Example 2:

Date ....

The problem is ....

....

To solve this problem I will

....

....

....

Signed

Pupil ....

Parent ....

36

7. Extracurricular activities

The extracurricular programme forms an integral part of the school programme. It includes all the activities that are not included in the formal curriculum. However, it should not be seen as separate from the formal curriculum. Participation in extracurricular activities is very important for a balanced education.

Extracurricular activities are usually voluntary but you should encourage your child to take part in at least one activity because they provide opportunities for:
* using leisure time in a constructive way;
* pursuing hobbies and interests;
* improving confidence and self-esteem;
* meeting new people and making new friends;
* getting to know others better;
* developing leadership skills;
* specialising in a field in which he or she shows a particular talent;
* developing a variety of skills;
* helping children develop a sense of responsibility;
* exposing children to a variety of experiences;
* developing team building; and
* acquiring new knowledge.

Types of activities

There are a wide variety of activities from which pupils can choose. Children should be encouraged to choose an activity that matches their interests and abilities.

These are some of the activities which could form part of an extracurricular programme:
* **Sports activities:** athletics, badminton, baseball, basketball, canoeing, cricket, hockey, netball, rugby, soccer, swimming, tennis, volley ball, and waterpolo
* **Music**
* **Art**
* **Drama.** School and house plays
* **Choir**

- **Clubs and societies.** Chess, computer, cookery, crafts, film, pottery, photography
- **Business games**
- **Community service**
- **School outings and excursions.** Some of the school outings are compulsory because they form an integral part of the academic curriculum.

Safety and supervision

All extracurricular activities must be supervised by staff members at all times. During these activities teachers are responsible for the safety of the pupils. The teacher on duty has to be fully aware of potential dangers and to provide guidance to pupils with regard to safety rules which should be observed at all times. Teachers who fail to supervise activities can be held liable for accidents which might occur.

It is recognised, however, that certain sports do involve some element of risk, and the child and his or her parents must be made aware of these risks and agree to the possibility of injury, provided the game is played according to the rules. It is important for the school to obtain permission from parents if their child is going to participate in a potentially dangerous sport, such as rugby or canoeing. In the event of an accident the parent will not be able to claim damages as long as the person responsible took the necessary precautions and there was no negligence involved.

Medical aid and medical treatment

Parents are generally required to cover all medical expenses in a case where their child has been injured. Schools only have limited medical insurance for pupils, parents and teachers who are being transported to and from a school outing. Parents need to ensure that their own medical aid policy covers their children. Those who do not have medical aid should discuss the matter with the principal.

Normally, parents have to give their consent before a child may receive medical treatment required as a result of a school activity. It is very important for parents to provide this consent, and to give the school details of any medical condition or special medical need of any of their children. The school should also have telephone numbers where parents or care-takers can be contacted.

Getting involved

Extracurricular activities provide a valuable opportunity for you to become involved in your child's schooling, and to play an active role in the school. If you do have an interest or skill in a particular sport why not offer to help the school when you can? Don't wait to be asked, rather approach the principal or teacher concerned and state your willingness to help. This could be in the early evening just after work, or during weekends, if you work full-time. If you cannot help with coaching, you can support the school and your child by doing the following:
- encourage your child to participate in an activity;
- keep a record of your child's activity programme;
- make sure your child has the correct clothes, equipment and/or materials;
- support your child's activity whenever possible;
- motivate your child by praising his or her efforts and achievements; and
- encourage your child to fulfil his or her commitment to the activity in which he or she is participating.

You can also help the school by:
- organising activities, such as sports days, competitions or outings;
- assisting with transport;

- coaching sport;
- catering for functions;
- fund-raising;
- assisting with the supervision of activities;
- running a club or society;
- attending and supporting school activities; and
- doing administrative tasks, such as typing letters, invitations or pro-grammes, contacting parents and distributing information.

Cancellation of activities

Pupils and parents must be given adequate notice of the cancellation of any activities so that they can make the necessary transport or other arrangements. At no time should pupils be left unattended or stranded as a result of cancellations.

Missing school to participate in extracurricular activities

If your child needs to be absent from school to take part in local, national or international activities, it is necessary to obtain permission from the principal. Arrangements should also be made regarding tests that your child might miss. He or she will be expected to make up work that is missed as a result of participation in such activities.

8. School trips and transport

School trips and visits to places of interest are a valuable form of enrichment of a child's education. These may take the form of day trips or those which extend over a number of days. The main aim of school trips is to make what the pupils learn at school more meaningful and interesting, to provide opportunities for children to see and experience new things, and extend their knowledge about their country and about the world around them. School trips may be planned to illustrate a particular section of a subject – for example a visit to a history museum, or as an extracurricular experience for general educational purposes, such as a visit to the Kruger National Park.

Safety and supervision

The teachers who accompany children on a school outing are responsible for their care and safety, and must take reasonable precautions during the trip. If a trip involves potentially dangerous activities, such as mountain climbing or canoeing, extra care must be taken. Teachers and instructors who are responsible for conducting these kinds of activities must be suitably qualified.

Good discipline is essential for safety. Rules should be made and clearly communicated to the pupils. The consequences of breaking the rules should also be clearly understood. You can support the teacher(s) by informing your children of your expectations as far as behaviour is concerned, and by drawing their attention to possible dangers and the importance of safety.

Is my consent needed?

It is the duty of the school to inform parents of school trips and to obtain your permission. This is usually done in the form of a letter giving details of the trip. A tear-off section is normally attached for parents to sign and return to the school. These slips should always be completed and returned to avoid problems. Schools can refuse to allow children to go on a trip if they do not have their parents' permission. This can cause a great deal of disappointment for the child. Whenever your child goes on a school trip, especially an extended trip, it is also important to give your consent for any necessary medical treatment, and to provide the school with details concerning your child's state of health.

Example of a consent form

Date ....

I have read the details for the school visit to

....

and I agree to my son/daughter taking part.

Signed ....

(Parent/guardian)

Do I need to sign indemnity forms?

When schools ask parents for permission to take their children on a school trip, they often expect them to sign an indemnity form to exempt the school from responsibility in the case of accidents and injuries, and protect themselves against any legal action. Although this is common practice, an indemnity will not protect the school in the case of negligence.

The following two points should be noted:
• Provided there is no negligence on the part of the school authorities and teachers, neither the principal, teacher, school governing body nor the education authorities are liable for injuries sustained by pupils.
• An indemnity only protects teachers and authorities if the responsible person acted in a reasonable and sensible manner. If a pupil is injured as a result of gross negligence or intentional misconduct, the indemnity will not exclude liability.

Letters of indemnity or exemption, therefore, do not release schools from their legal duty to care for the pupils in their charge nor do they protect schools in the case of negligence. Parents should, therefore, not be forced to sign forms that absolve the school from their normal responsibility in caring for the child.

Is the school covered by insurance?

In general, schools will carry a certain amount of insurance to cover pupils and staff. Before your child goes on a trip, check to see if the school is adequately insured. You should also make sure that your personal insurance for your child is adequate.

Important data

The following is a list of details which parents should know about each school trip:
- Nature and purpose of journey
- The number of teachers accompanying the pupils
- The names of the teachers accompanying the pupils
- Type of transport to be used
- Destination
- Departure and arrival times
- Cost to the parents
- Medical provisions that will be available
- Contact telephone numbers
- Clothing and other requirements.

School Journey Services

The School Journey Services assist schools with arranging school outings and excursions. The aim of study tours is to supplement the syllabus content and to make it more relevant and interesting. The School Journey Services will advise schools on places to visit and requirements, and will assist them in compiling itineraries. Schools are usually required to arrange the transport (which must meet the requirements of the Road Traffic Act) and insurance cover.

9. Financial matters

Most schools require parents to pay school fees and also to pay for other items such as books and school outings. School fees vary from school to school. They can be as little as R250,00 a year, or as much as R2 400,00 a year or even more. Private schools are much more expensive than state and state-aided schools.

School fees are compulsory for pupils attending state-aided schools and private schools, and the school governing body has the legal power to set and collect school fees. If parents fail to pay the school fees, legal action can be taken against them. However, if they cannot or do not pay school fees, the matter must be taken up with the parents directly and not with the child. The child may not be discriminated against or humiliated in any way. School fees should not be discussed with pupils in the presence of other pupils. Children may also not be sent home, have books taken away or material withheld if their parents do not pay school fees. School fees should be collected in a tactful way.

In the case of state schools, school fees are not compulsory. Parents are, however, usually asked to contribute towards a school fund. Although parents cannot be forced to contribute and in no way may the child be prejudiced, parents are encouraged to support the school fund because it is essential for maintaining good teaching facilities.

State subsidy

Financial subsidies are available to parents who cannot afford school fees. There are, however, certain requirements that must be met before a subsidy can be granted. Parents of pupils who live in the feeder area, that is the area in which the school is situated and serves, may apply for a subsidy to help pay for school fees. Application forms for a state subsidy are obtainable from the principal of the school.

Personal details, including proof of earnings, must be furnished. The amount of the subsidy will depend on the family's annual income. For example, a family with an annual income of R35 000 and over is not eligible for a subsidy. A subsidy is also granted on a sliding scale, which means that the lower the annual income the greater the subsidy will be. There is, however, a maximum subsidy which can be received for each child.

Educational bursaries

Educational bursaries for secondary and tertiary education are available from various organisations.

An educational bursary is:
- a form of financial assistance;
- made available to students who are unable to pay for their education;
- awarded on the basis of merit and academic results.

Tips on applying for a bursary
Bursaries are available from various sources, including educational institutions, companies, industry, private organisations and church groups.

These steps should be followed when applying for a bursary.
- Approach the schools, universities, colleges and education departments for information on the availability of bursaries
- Decide what kind of bursary your child needs
- Establish what the requirements are for each bursary
- Help your child apply for several bursaries, but only accept one
- Submit the applications well in advance
- Ensure that your child's application is neat and accurate.

10. Discipline and punishment

Good discipline at school is essential for creating and maintaining a positive learning environment. All schools have a disciplinary policy that sets out the rules and expectations for pupil behaviour. Disciplinary policies may vary from school to school because of the different approaches to maintaining discipline and punishing pupils. It is, therefore, a sensible idea to obtain a copy of the code of discipline of your child's school so that you know what is expected of him or her and can support this policy at home.

School rules

School rules normally deal with matters such as attendance, punctuality, uniforms, behaviour, use of premises and school work. You should make sure that your child knows and understands the rules, and is fully aware of the consequences of breaking them. School rules are drawn up by the principal in consultation with the teachers and the school governing body. They should not be in conflict with general school policy or any regulation set out by the education departments. School rules are required to be in writing and made known to pupils and parents. If any of the rules are not clear or are ambiguous, you should obtain clarity from the principal.

Punishment

Although principals and teachers have the legal power to administer punishment, this power is not unlimited. There are certain legal rules and regulations which guide and control the use of punishment. There are many different forms of punishment that teachers can apply which do not have specific legal requirements other than that they must be fair and reasonable, such as being kept in at break, writing lines or cleaning the playground. Detention, corporal punishment, suspension and expulsion are more serious forms of punishment and are regulated by law. All parents should be aware of the rules regarding these forms of punishment.

Detention

This is probably the most common form of serious punishment. Pupils can be detained during break-time or after school. If a child is kept in after school, both the child and the parents should be given fair warning so that adequate arrangements can be made for transport and supervision. Parents should be told what time their child will be permitted to leave school.

In some cases it is impossible for pupils to remain after school. If your child has been instructed to stay in after school and it is not possible for you to make suitable arrangements, you are free to discuss the matter with the teacher concerned. It is quite possible that a different form of punishment may be used. Children in detention must be supervised and given constructive work to do.

Corporal punishment

There is a great deal of debate and controversy about the use of corporal punishment. Many parents are opposed to their children being physically beaten. Others approve of the practice. In spite of the different opinions on the matter, the law does allow the use of corporal punishment in certain circumstances.

Corporal punishment is seen as a last resort to be used only for serious offences, such as chronic truancy, bullying, vandalism, physical assault and theft. Leaving a book at home or failing to complete a homework assignment does not warrant corporal punishment. In terms of common law, punishment should be fair and reasonable.

The following aspects should be taken into consideration before administering corporal punishment:
* the age of the child;
* the physical and emotional state of the child;
* the nature of the offence;
* the purpose of the punishment.

Statutory laws regulate the administering of corporal punishment. The provisions of the law are summarised as follows:
* only the principal or a person authorised to do so in writing, or a teacher authorised to do so in the presence of the principal, may administer corporal punishment;
* corporal punishment may not be administered to girls;
* corporal punishment may not be administered to pre-primary and junior primary pupils;

- corporal punishment may not be administered to handicapped pupils without the approval of a medical officer;
- the principal is required to keep a register recording the administering of corporal punishment and the reason for the punishment;
- corporal punishment may not be administered to pupils in the presence of other pupils.

The education laws on corporal punishment do vary slightly from one education department to another, so it is worthwhile to check with the school to determine what its policy is.

Suspension

A child may be barred from school for a period of time if he or she has committed a very serious offence. Principals can only suspend a pupil after consultation with the Superintendent of Education (or equivalent), and the child's parents. Parents should be notified immediately of the offence and the reasons for the suspension. They must be given a chance to discuss the matter with the principal and to give their reasons for not supporting the suspension. In some cases the suspension can be reversed.

Expulsion

Like suspension, expulsion is only used in extreme cases because of the grave consequences it has for the child's future. A pupil can only be expelled if the Executive Director gives his or her permission. Once the decision to expel a pupil is made, the principal should inform the pupil and the parents in writing, and a report must be submitted to the Executive Director of Education. The parents' views should also be conveyed in the report.

In private schools, the authority to suspend and expel pupils lies with the principal and/or school governing body. If your child attends a private school, make sure that you are informed about the school's disciplinary policy on suspension and expulsion, and that you and your child know what offences can lead to suspension and/or expulsion.

The right to due process

The right to due process is a legal concept which means that an individual must be given the opportunity to present his side of the story in his defence. Therefore, if a child is being punished, he or she must be given the chance to state his or her case. This is particularly important in more serious cases of breach of discipline, such as those which could lead to suspension or expulsion. In this regard parents also have a right to due process and must be given an opportunity to put their case to the principal or school governing body. This prevents any arbitrary or unfair practice on the part of the school.

11. Parents as partners

It is generally accepted that parents are an integral part of the schooling process, and that their participation in school activities is necessary for effective schooling.

There are many ways in which parents can become involved in the school and thus in the education of their children.

Parents as governors

The law makes provision for the establishment of a school governing body consisting of the principal and parents elected by the parent community. The function of this governing body is to represent the parents and help the principal with the day-to-day management of the school. Serving on the governing body gives parents the opportunity to make a meaningful contribution towards their children's education.

The governing body fulfils a number of important tasks, which include:
* drawing up the school budget;
* managing the school's finances;
* collecting school fees;
* raising funds;
* appointing staff;
* maintaining school buildings and grounds; and
* organising school functions.

Many parents who serve on the governing body do so voluntarily and this work is usually in addition to their normal occupations. The governing body therefore needs the support of the entire parent body.

Election of the governing body

One person, known as a returning officer, is appointed to arrange the election of the members of the governing body. The returning officer may appoint one or more persons to assist him or her with this election. The first step is to inform parents of the meeting at which candidates are to be nominated. Any parent who has a child at the school is entitled to vote at an election meeting, and can also be elected to serve on the school governing body.

Each prospective candidate must be proposed by one parent and seconded by another. A nomination form must be completed in respect of each candidate. The forms are available from the principal prior to the meeting, and they are also available at the meeting. If there are more nominations than the number required for the committee, a poll is held to allow parents to vote for a candidate. Each parent who wishes to vote is given a ballot paper on which he or she indicates his or her choice.

At the first meeting of the governing body, the members elect a chairman and vice-chairman. The term of office is valid for the duration of the school year.

Meetings of the governing body

If you are elected to serve on the governing body, you will be required to attend several meetings during the course of the year. Members are advised of the meetings in writing. The secretary of the governing body takes minutes of the meetings and circulates copies to each member.

Parent-teacher associations

Many schools have parent-teacher associations or committees which are non-statutory bodies, that is, they are non-legal bodies and they do not have any legal powers. All parents usually automatically become members of the parent-teacher association, or PTA. Parent-teacher associations serve to encourage the educational partnership between the home and school for the benefit of the children. They provide a forum for educational discussion and a means of communication between the home and the school. They also co-ordinate and arrange a variety of school functions and activities. One of their responsibilities is to keep parents informed on matters pertaining to the school.

Any parent can volunteer to serve on a parent-teacher association. If you are unable to or do not wish to be on a committee, you can support the parent-teacher association in many other ways: for example, by occasionally helping to organise functions or simply by attending and supporting these functions. You could also offer to serve as a contact person in your community, and liaise between the parent-teacher association and parents living in a particular area. This facilitates communication between the school and the parent community.

Class committees

Some schools have a parent-class committee. This kind of committee is very informal, and is a very effective way of bringing together parents of children in the same class or standard. Parent-class committees provide opportunities for parents to get to know each other, to meet the teachers on an informal basis and to support each other in various educational endeavours. Each parent representing a particular class could, for example, arrange an afternoon or evening during the year to invite the other parents to his or her home or to the school for an informal get-together. This is also an ideal way for parents to keep track of what their children are doing and to collaborate on matters that concern their children!

Parents as helpers

Many parents are not able to or do not wish to serve on a formal committee, but they can help in other ways. There are many things a parent can do to help the school without feeling overburdened. A parent may, for example:
- help with playground duty;
- take a turn to serve in the tuckshop;

- help with extracurricular activities;
- help to raise funds;
- assist with the organisation of school functions;
- assist in the school library;
- help compile the school magazine;
- translate newsletters into the parents' home languages;
- do repair and maintenance jobs;
- help with the gardening;
- accompany teachers on school trips;
- contact other parents about important school events;
- arrange parent talks and information sessions in the afternoons and evenings;
- help with school concerts;
- attend school functions; and
- serve as an interpreter for non-English speaking parents.

Parents as classroom aides

There are many ways in which parents can help teachers in the classroom, especially in the junior primary classes. Some parents can help the teacher by spending time in the classroom listening to the children read, and reading to them. Parents can help with setting out equipment, cutting out pictures, doing illustrations for worksheets, handing out work, supervising games and teaching children songs.

Although having parents to help in the classroom works very well during the junior and senior primary phases, there are also ways in which parents can be of assistance in the high school. Many parents who are experts or specialists in a particular field can be invited to give talks to pupils – for example, parents with a particular knowledge in the field of science, nature conservation, art and so on. Parents who are experts in the field of computer science can be invited to help with teaching computer studies in the evenings. If you are an expert in a particular field or have a specific skill, such as carpentry, do offer your services to the school.

Parents who are working full-time and do not have much time to spare, can also offer to spend a little time in the evenings covering books, cutting out pictures or making posters. It is important, however, to remember that you are there to help the teacher and not to do his or her work. The teacher should be in the classroom all the time to provide the parent with the necessary information and guidance.

54

How to get involved

Often parents want to help but they do not know what they can do or how to go about offering their services. Parents often wait to be asked by the school, instead of going directly to the principal or teacher to offer assistance.

Try the following:
- let the school know that you are interested and willing to help in any way you can. Take the opportunity to tell the principal and teachers this when you have occasion to talk to them;
- if the school sends a note home requesting help from parents, return the note indicating what you can and are prepared to do. Give an indication of the times when you are available to help.

Parent workshops

Some schools hold regular talks, information sessions and workshops for parents. This is, however, only done on a small scale. More schools should be encouraged to hold talks and workshops for parents on a variety of topics. Parents can also play a very important role in helping to arrange talks, seminars and workshops throughout the year. A special committee could be formed to fulfil this function.

The following topics are suggested for talks and workshops:
- working with the underachiever;
- dealing with learning problems;
- effective study skills;
- helping your child prepare for matric;
- understanding the child with an attention deficit disorder;
- health care;
- parent-child reading programmes;
- new developments in education;
- sex education;
- multicultural education;
- supporting language development;
- supervising your child's homework;
- effective communication with your child;
- motivating your child; and
- the school curriculum.

12. Effective communication with the school

Open communication is essential for maintaining good relationships with the school and your child's teachers. Often misunderstandings and incorrect impressions arise because of poor or infrequent communication between parents and teachers.

Making personal contact

It is very important for your child's education that you should have regular personal contact with his or her teachers. Schools usually arrange special parent-teacher evenings during the course of the year so that parents can meet teachers and discuss their children's work. Attend these meetings whenever possible. However, these meetings offer only a limited opportunity for meaningful communication. If you are unable to attend the scheduled meetings or you wish to see the teachers more frequently, make an appointment for a time that suits both you and the teacher, and gives you sufficient time to discuss matters concerning your child's education.

It is also not advisable to wait for the scheduled parent-teacher evenings to discuss new problems. These are best dealt with when they arise. Do not wait for the problem to reach a crisis stage before you contact the teacher. If you are concerned about any aspect of your child's education, contact the school immediately.

Telephone calls

One of the most effective and efficient means of communication is the telephone, and yet it not used as often as it could. Many parents do not feel comfortable about telephoning teachers at home.

Occasions do, however, arise where it might be necessary for you to telephone a teacher at his or her home, and this is quite acceptable. On the other hand, telephone calls to teachers during teaching time should be avoided. It is always good policy to telephone the secretary and find out when the teacher will be available and the most convenient time to telephone. The secretary can then tell the teacher to expect your call, or the teacher can return your call at his or her convenience. If you need to telephone the principal or a teacher at home, choose a reasonable time.

Know exactly what you want to say and keep the conversation as brief as possible. Write down the information or questions before telephoning so that you do not forget what you want to say or leave out anything important. When making the call state clearly why you are telephoning. Always be polite but speak with confidence. Avoid being over-apologetic.

Here are a few examples of brief openers after you have introduced yourself:

Mrs Jones, I am phoning because:
- I am concerned about Mark's poor report;
- I am concerned that Graeme has not received any homework for several weeks.
- I am worried about Michelle. Lately she has been coming home from school very depressed.
- I just want to let you know that Laura is in hospital having her appendix removed and will not be at school for one week.

Formal letters

Formal letters written to the principal or teacher should be neatly written or typed, as well as being accurate, polite and to the point. If you are not sure of what to say, or if you need to write in a language which is not your first language, it is advisable to ask a family member, friend or colleague to assist you with the content and language.

Personal notes and cards

There are many occasions during the course of the year that provide ideal opportunities for parents to make contact with the teacher through brief letters, notes and cards. These notes do not need to be formal, neither do they have to be specially bought. A neatly-written hand-made card is appreciated just as much as an expensive one. Letters should be clear and to the point. Address the teacher by name whenever possible, e.g. Mrs Jones, and identify your child in the letter so that the teacher knows whom the letter concerns.

When to send notes
Notes may be sent under the following circumstances:
- Notes should be sent to teachers when a child is sick and has to be absent from school. This is particularly important in view of the fact that schools are required to keep a register of pupils' attendance and

absenteeism. If your child has been absent for three or more days, you may be requested to furnish a doctor's certificate.

- A thank-you note or card can be sent to teachers as a gesture of appreciation for the work they do. You do not have to wait for a special occasion. A simple note of thanks and appreciation during the course of the year is always appreciated, especially if a teacher has taken special trouble to assist your child in some way. This may have meant staying after school to give extra tuition or supervision to help him or her catch up with the work.
- Cards can also be sent to teachers on special occasions. If you know the date of your child's teacher's birthday you can send a card. Let your child make a card and send it from the whole family. Making cards is less expensive, which is an important factor if your child is in high school and has several teachers.

Here are some examples of informal letters.

Dear Mrs Paton

Thank you for helping Samantha catch up the work she missed while she was ill. She really appreciated it.

Sincerely

Mrs Goodley

Dear Mr Bailey

Ephraim was so pleased that his soccer team won the the trophy. Thank you for your excellent coaching.

Many thanks

Mr and Mrs Kumalo

Dear Ms Donald

Please excuse Petro from taking part in the physical education class today because she has pulled a muscle in her back. She is being treated by her doctor.

Thanking you

Mrs Meiring

Dear Mr Potter

My son Ahmed has been absent for two days with an ear infection.

Yours sincerely

Mr Reddy

Notes and letters addressing sensitive issues

Often parents use their children's homework diaries to write notes and comments on sensitive issues, or include queries they might have about the teacher's or child's work. This is not at all advisable. If there is something to which you would like to draw the teacher's attention, or something you wish to query, either make an appointment and discuss the matter face-to-face with the teacher or write a friendly, polite but confidential letter. Some schools may have a special diary for pupils to carry, in which teachers and parents may write notes and messages.

Examples:

Dear Ms Kemp

While I was helping Paula with her health test on diseases, I read a sentence on viruses that appears to be incorrect. I would be grateful if this could be checked.

Sincerely

Mrs Dutton

Dear Mrs Clarke

Karen has been given a geography worksheet to complete for homework. I have, however, noticed several typing errors on the worksheet which appear to have been overlooked.

Yours sincerely

Mrs Poole

Receiving letters and newsletters

Schools normally send out letters, circulars, memos and newsletters to parents on a regular basis. It is important to read these and to respond to them whenever you are asked to do so. Keep important letters and circulars in a file in a safe place for future reference.

Home visits

Some schools encourage home visits. This provides an opportunity for teachers to visit parents and pupils at home, especially when parents are unable to get to the school. Parents are often wary of home visits by teachers because they feel it is an invasion of their privacy. However, home visits can have very positive results and can be rewarding for both the teacher and family if they are conducted in a spirit of co-operation and mutual respect, and on the understanding that the teacher is merely visiting the child's home in everyone's best interests. Through home visits, parents and teachers can get to know one another on a more personal level. Home visits are particularly useful for working with parents of pre-primary and junior primary pupils, and parents of children with special needs.

13. Getting the most out of parent-teacher meetings

At least twice a year schools hold parent-teacher evenings for parents to visit the teachers to discuss their children's work. Often parents are given only a very short time to talk to the teacher and they leave feeling dissatisfied because they have not been able to have a meaningful conversation. Also, the fact that these meetings are usually held in the early evening makes it impossible for some parents to attend. How can you as a parent deal with this situation?

You should make every effort to attend these meetings whenever possible. If you have problems, such as not having transport or not being able to get hold of a baby-sitter, contact the school and find out if they are able to assist in any way. Some schools will arrange for other parents to assist with transport, and it may also be possible for the school to arrange for someone to look after your children in a classroom while you are talking to the teacher. If it is really impossible to attend the meeting, make an appointment to see the teachers on another day. It is important for you to meet your child's teachers to discuss his or her work and progress.

Being prepared beforehand

To make the best use of the limited time available it is necessary to be well prepared for your discussion with the teacher. Decide what you want to find out from the teacher. Write down the questions you wish to ask, and list them in order of their importance so that if you are unable to ask them all you will at least have asked the most important ones. Those remaining can be asked at a later stage. Writing down the questions will also help you to remember important details. Ask each question clearly and insist on specific answers.

The broad categories given on the diagram on the next page will help you formulate meaningful questions and obtain useful information:

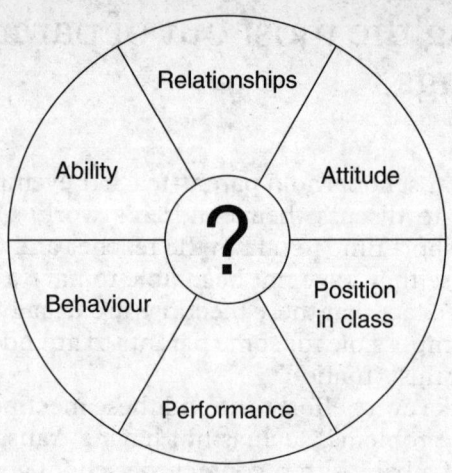

Here are some basic questions that you can ask:
- How is my child coping with his or her maths (or any other subject)?
- What group is my child in for reading?
- Is my child's spelling improving?
- Is my child completing classwork on time?
- May I please see some examples of my child's work?
- Does my child participate in class discussion and group activities?
- How is my child's behaviour in class?
- Is my child making friends?
- How much homework should my child be doing each day?
- What weekly test should my child be studying for? On what days do they write tests?
- What particular skills does my child need to develop or improve?
- How can I help my child at home?
- Has my child's science (or any other subject) improved?

Questions can also be more specific. For example:

Parent: I noticed that my daughter was given a demerit for untidy work. Is her work generally untidy? How can we help?

Parent: I notice from my son's books that his writing is very poor and even though his work is very accurate he is being penalised for his writing. How can we help him improve his writing?

Parent: I am very concerned about the many negative comments that are written in my child's book. She is becoming very demotivated. Why is she getting these comments and how can we help improve the situation?

If you are unable to obtain all the information you require because of insufficient time, or if you feel no conclusions have been reached or solutions found, make another appointment for as soon as possible afterwards. Never leave a problem unresolved, because this will not help your child to succeed at school.

Giving information

At parent-teacher meetings it is just as important to give the teacher information as it is to receive it. You are in a position to provide teachers with valuable details about your child that will help them know and understand him or her better. If you think that certain information will help the teacher to understand and cope with your child, make sure that you pass it on to the teacher. For example, your child might be on specific medication which could be affecting his or her work. Remember to also give positive information: for example, your child might have received a medal or certificate in recognition of some achievement in an after-school activity.

Important information that you can give to the teacher
- Mention any noticeable changes in your child's behaviour.
- Mention what your child does well.
- Let the teacher know when there is tension in the family or any other problems, such as a divorce, death of a friend or family member, illness, retrenchment, change in jobs, moving house, death of a pet and so on.
- Mention your child's achievements in after-school activities.

Guidelines for effective parent-teacher meetings
- Be well prepared.
- Know the name(s) of your child's teacher(s).
- Study your child's report before going to the meeting.
- Arrive on time for the meeting.
- Ask questions.
- Give information about your child.
- Be positive.
- Avoid getting angry. Stay calm.

Coping with conflict

There are occasions when parents have to see a teacher or principal about a problem which could give rise to a conflict situation. The kinds of situation which could cause conflict between parent and teacher or parent and principal are these:
- your child is failing and you are unhappy about the way in which the teacher is teaching him or her;
- your child is being subjected to corporal punishment;
- your child is playing truant;
- your child is continuously being punished for not doing homework but no one has contacted you to discuss the problem;
- your child seems to have a learning problem but little is being done to help him or her or discuss it with you, and so on.

When many parents have to go to the school to deal with any of these problems, they are often at a disadvantage because they feel threatened or intimidated, especially if the attitude of the principal or teachers appears to be superior and condescending. You should remind yourself that you have a right to be concerned about your child's education and are entitled to discuss any matter which concerns it. Your status, qualifications or occupation are irrelevant in such a case. All parents, no matter what their circumstances, should be treated with equal respect and dignity.

The best way to deal with difficult situations which have the potential for conflict is to be well prepared and to keep calm. Always try to make an appointment which will last long enough to discuss the matter in full. Avoid unscheduled visits as this can lead to frustration and aggravate the situation if the teacher or principal is not available. Remember that teachers may not leave their classes unattended to discuss matters with parents.

In some cases it is useful to first write to the principal expressing your concern and requesting an appointment. This will give the principal time to investigate the matter before seeing you.

When you meet the principal or teacher be clear in your own mind about what you want to say and what you hope to achieve. Make sure that you have all the necessary facts and information. Maintain a positive attitude and avoid making accusing statements. You must also be prepared to listen to what the principal or teacher has to say. It is vitally important to stay focused on the issue. Do not get sidetracked or allow the matter to be pushed aside unresolved. Make sure that you leave the meeting on a positive note, with the matter resolved. If necessary, schedule another appointment to follow up on the issue.

14. Children with special needs

The term "special needs" is used here to refer to children who, for different reasons, require some modification to or adaptation of their educational environment and learning programme to help them achieve. Children differ in respect of a number of factors, such as ability, interests, physical development, emotional level and aptitude. They do not all develop at the same rate or reach school-readiness at the same age.

Many children also have special learning needs. For example: some children might have poor hearing, visual problems, a speech impediment or a specific learning problem such as dyslexia. Others might even need to attend special schools, such as a school for the blind.

No matter what the situation, the school system needs to provide an education appropriate to the needs of all children. Children with special needs can only be helped and supported if the parents and school work closely together. The school plays a very important role in identifying problems and needs, and in providing expert advice. Parents need to follow up on the school's advice and provide the necessary feedback to the school.

The learning-disabled child

"Learning disability" is a general term used to describe a heterogeneous group of disorders that are manifested by significant difficulty in the acquisition and use of listening, reading, writing, speaking, reasoning or mathematical skills (Hallahan & Kauffmann 1991). Conditions classified as learning disabilities include dyslexia, perceptual handicaps and neurological and educational impairment. Learning-disabled children therefore experience particular difficulty in one or more academic areas. The causes of learning disabilities are not known conclusively. There are various factors – which may be genetic, biological or environmental – that can cause learning disabilities.

If a child does have a learning disability, early diagnosis and intervention are important to prevent problems later on and to ensure that the child is provided with the correct educational programme. If learning disabilities are ignored, the child is at great risk of failing and possibly dropping out of school.

It is essential, therefore, for parents and teachers to work closely together to support the learning-disabled child. If your child is diagnosed as having a learning disability, it is very important for you to liaise with the teacher and specialists, and to follow their advice. Children with a learning disability should receive suitably adapted education which will enable them to cope and succeed at school.

The underachiever

Often children who are expected to perform well at school fail to achieve. These children are often labelled "lazy" and "a problem". It is important for teachers and parents to identify the underachiever and to determine the reasons for the child's poor performance. Teachers and parents should work together to encourage and support such a child, and to help him or her reach his or her fullest possible potential.

Reasons for underachieving
Some of the reasons that might contribute to a child's underachievement are outlined below:
- Physical illness can affect a child's ability to concentrate and learn. Long illness can result in missing work and falling behind.
- Emotional distress caused by various incidents, such as a death in the family or violence in the community, can also prevent a child from learning effectively.
- Malnutrition can result in a child not having the necessary physical strength to work properly. This can lead to poor concentration and the inability to attend in class. Malnutrition can also lead to other physical problems, such as poor eyesight, which in turn affect learning.
- Medication can also affect performance. Certain drugs can lower a child's concentration and attention span.
- Unrealistic expectations on the part of the parent or teacher can result in a child underachieving when he or she is pressurised. Parents and teachers should have realistic expectations of what the child can achieve and then encourage and motivate him or her to succeed.
- Undermining a child's ability can have a negative affect on his or her performance. Telling a child that he or she is slow, useless, stupid or not very bright, or simply doubting his or her ability, can lead to the development of a very negative self-image. The child will eventually believe that he or she is stupid and give up trying to do well. It will also be very difficult for him or her to overcome feelings of inadequa-

cy and inferiority. Teachers should also never belittle a child in front of other children. If you are aware of this happening, discuss the matter with the principal immediately.

- A poor teacher-pupil relationship can affect a child's ability to perform well. A child who does not like, or is afraid of, his or her teacher, is likely to develop a negative attitude to the subject taught by this teacher and is less likely to do well.
- A lack of interest in the subject does not enhance learning. Children who do not enjoy a subject tend to spend less time on it and put in less effort.

The gifted child

In the past, children with special needs have usually been regarded as having learning disabilities and physical handicaps, and special services and schools have been established for them. Gifted children have special needs arising from specific abilities. Gifted children also often experience educational, social and emotional problems, and for this reason they also need counselling and guidance to help them deal with their giftedness and to alleviate pressures that might arise from being gifted.

Gifted children are often left to work things out for themselves, are sometimes rejected by their peers and their relationships with adults and siblings can be awkward. They are often aware of being different and may experience feelings of alienation. They therefore need the support of family and friends who understand their special needs.

What, actually, is a gifted child? There are many definitions of giftedness but experts agree that a gifted child is one who is exceptionally capable in several areas and is both a high achiever and an outstanding performer. Gifted children tend to excel at school and obtain very high grades in all subjects. They are generally at the top of their class and standard. Because gifted children are able to master the standard of work required very quickly, they need more advanced and challenging work, as well as special educational programmes. Those who are not given challenging and enriching tasks, are at risk of becoming bored and frustrated.

A gifted child can become an underachiever if he or she is not provided with the right kind of stimulation and experiences. For this reason, various strategies have been used to meet the needs of the gifted child. These include advancement to the next standard, extracurricular enrichment programmes, independent study programmes and special programmes for gifted children. There are a number of centres for gifted children attached to colleges of education, which offer a variety of study programmes. Parents have an important role to play in supporting their child who has been identified as being gifted, by maintaining open communication with the teachers, providing appropriate stimulation and encouraging him or her to take up interesting and challenging hobbies.

How do you know if your child is gifted? Identifying giftedness is not a straightforward matter: parents and teachers play an important role in identifying gifted children but it is important for children who display the characteristics of giftedness, to be tested by professional people. Identification is multifaceted and involves a variety of intelligence, achievement and creativity tests.

Extra tuition

Extra classes after school hours can benefit a child who requires a special educational programme. Extra classes are often needed because a teacher's time and resources are limited during normal school hours. Teachers should do all they can to enhance each child's learning and to provide suitable learning experiences, but they are required to teach large classes of pupils with varying needs.

Teachers and parents of children with special needs should work together to design and implement appropriate educational programmes. Parents can provide teachers with important information about their children, and this should be taken into account when planning extra tuition. However, these children should not be overburdened with extra classes and additional tuition to the extent that it prevents them from enjoying their leisure time, participating in hobbies and interacting with friends. It is important to create a balance in a child's life.

Specialist services and support groups

There are specialist services and support groups to help parents and children with special needs. A list of some of these services is given in Appendix A on page 99. These specialist services and support groups can give emotional support and provide one with essential information.

Educational aid services

These services play a very important role in counselling and testing children, and providing professional guidance to children, parents and teachers on various matters.

Educational aid centres are staffed by professionals who are able to assist children who are experiencing social, emotional and learning problems. The educational aid services develop special programmes to suit the needs of each child, depending on the nature of the problem. There is no stigma attached to the use of these services: they are essential educational support services.

You can approach your child's school for more details on services which are available in your area. The telephone numbers of the various educational aid centres are listed in the telephone directory. There are also many private practices which can be found in the telephone directories. Your doctor will also be able to refer you to professional people who will be able to help and advise you on the needs of your child.

Welfare services

Nowadays children are faced with many social problems, such as alcoholism, drug abuse, child abuse, broken homes and violence in the community. These problems can have a very negative effect on a child and his or her achievement at school. There are a variety of welfare organisations that work with schools on an informal basis to counsel, advise and support pupils, parents and teachers.

15. Medical matters

Children are prone to a wide range of medical problems which can interrupt learning and have a negative effect on their performance at school. Medical problems can range from minor temporary illnesses to more long-term, serious illnesses, or permanent conditions which have to be closely monitored and treated, such as diabetes and epilepsy. If your child does have a medical condition it is very important that you inform the school and provide medical certificates and up-to-date information on the child's condition and progress. Provide the school with all the details regarding the problem, how it affects your child and how it is to be treated. Make sure that the school has correct contact numbers to reach you in case of an emergency.

Medication

Many children are on medication for a long period of time or even permanently. Inform the school fully about the medication, and the dosages to be administered. It is worthwhile giving the school the name and telephone number of your doctor in case of an emergency.

Illness and school sport

There are certain regulations regarding a child's health and participation in physical activities. If your child has an illness or injury which prevents him or her from taking part in physical activities, inform the school in writing. Make sure that the physical education teacher and the sports coach have the information and that your child is formally excused from such activities.

School health services

The School Health Services fall under the control of the Department of National Health. The aim of these services is to promote health, to prevent physical and psychological disease and to create a healthy climate in schools. Health officials pay regular visits to schools: they carry out medical examinations, test eyesight and hearing, and administer vaccinations. Parents are informed of any medical conditions or problems their child might have, and are advised on the steps to be taken. This information should be followed up with your family doctor or the local clinic.

Immunisation

Infectious diseases can spread very easily in schools and it is therefore important to take all the necessary precautions to prevent your child from becoming ill or infecting others. It is also necessary to have your child immunised against diseases such as measles, diphtheria, rubella and tuberculosis. If your child has already been immunised and you do not wish him or her to be immunised again at school, inform the school in writing and provide a medical certificate to that effect.

Dental service

School children are also expected to undergo dental examinations. If you do not wish your child to have a dental examination at school it is again necessary to advise the school in writing. The school may require you to submit a certificate from your dentist.

Medical aid

Schools do not have medical aid cover for pupils. Parents are expected to pay for all medical expenses. If you do not have medical aid, you can consult the principal for advice on this matter.

Part II

Helping your child at home

There are many ways in which parents can help their children succeed at school. In this part of the book we look at the ways in which parents can support their children at home. This is particularly important for working parents who do not have the time or opportunity to visit the school and attend school functions on a regular basis.

16. Motivating your child

Children who are highly motivated generally feel good about themselves and do well at school. You can play an important role in motivating your child by helping to build up his or her self-esteem, giving effective praise and by being supportive and encouraging.

Building self-esteem

Children with a high self-esteem have a positive image of themselves, they like themselves, and feel confident and secure. They believe in their strengths and ability to cope with situations. A low self-esteem can have a negative effect on a child's work and performance at school. Children who are insecure, lack confidence and have a poor image of themselves, are inclined to do less well at school. It is also more difficult for them to make friends and join groups. Teachers often unconsciously spend less time with such children because they tend often to remain detached and keep to themselves. They are also at risk of going unnoticed.

Here are some ideas of how you can help your child develop his or her self-esteem:

- Listen to what your child has to say.
- Take time to talk to your child about his or her interests.
- Do not talk down to your child.
- Acknowledge and be sensitive to your child's opinions.
- Encourage your child to pursue a hobby that he or she enjoys and is good at.
- Avoid using ridicule and sarcasm.
- Labels such as lazy, stupid or slow, should never be used.
- Let your child know you support him or her.
- Demonstrate how much you care for your child.
- Share activities with your child.
- Give your child responsibility.
- Have realistic expectations of your child.
- Encourage your child to discuss problems with you.
- Encourage open and frank communication.
- Respect your child's privacy.
- Look for positive things to compliment your child on rather than remonstrate in a negative way.

Effective praise

Children of all ages need praise and recognition for their achievements. Giving effective praise can contribute towards building your child's self-esteem, confidence, motivation and success at school. However, for praise to be effective, it should be used in a careful and meaningful way.

Effective praise:
- is purposeful;
- is given only when it is merited;
- is simple, direct and sincere;
- is spontaneous;
- attributes success to ability and effort;
- provides children with information about their ability;
- encourages children to focus on their own efforts;
- names the actual accomplishment; and
- can be non-verbal, such as a pat on the shoulder or a nod of the head, as well as verbal.

Here are some praise comments that you can use to motivate your child. Think up other useful praise comments as well.
- I am proud of the way you completed your project.
- I enjoyed reading your essay. The plot is interesting.
- You really seemed to enjoy that story. You read with a lot of expression.
- This work is very accurate. Well done!
- That's an excellent observation.
- Your writing has improved. Keep it up!
- This work shows that you were concentrating.
- That's an interesting point you have made.
- Your picture shows good use of colour.
- You obtained a good mark in that test. I am very pleased.
- You have really worked hard at your homework.
- Well done! You managed to solve the problem on your own.
- This good mark shows that you have studied hard.

Motivation

Children must be motivated for them to succeed in school. Motivation can be external or internal. External motivation is when something outside the child encourages him or her to want to do something. For example: it might be the desire to win the school cup, to get a certificate for good work, to avoid punishment or simply to please the teacher. Internal motivation is usually a better incentive. Children are more likely to achieve and be successful if they are motivated from an inner desire to accomplish something successfully, irrespective of reward. In other words, they do something because it is for themselves, because they want to do it and enjoy doing it, and because they believe they are competent to do it. They derive personal satisfaction from their accomplishment.

Children are more easily motivated if:
- they are engaged in meaningful learning;
- the environment is secure and pleasant;
- they are rewarded for good performance;
- they have clear goals to work towards;
- learning tasks are adapted to their interests and experiences;
- they are given the opportunity to make choices;
- they are given appropriate feedback regarding their tasks; and
- they experience success.

The following are ways in which you can motivate your child.
- Help your child organise his or her time so that there is a balance between work and leisure time
- Help your child set goals that are attainable
- Reward your child for his or her achievement
- Show your child that you believe in his or her ability
- Help your child to understand and cope with failure.

Setting realistic goals

Pressure is often placed on children to achieve unrealistic goals which only serve to frustrate them and impede learning. If children are unable to achieve what is expected of them, they often simply give up and then run the risk of underachieving and even failing. If a child is struggling with maths and has been getting very low marks, say, 20%, he or she should not be pressurised to get 60% in the next test. Work out an appropriate plan of action and set a realistic goal. Even if the child only gets 40% in the next test it is still a 100% improvement and should be rewarded. Unfortunately rewards and merits are often based on the achievement of high marks rather than on improved performance, irrespective of the mark.

Setting realistic goals and rewarding children for achieving those goals is therefore important for helping them to succeed at school, to become motivated and to develop a positive self-image. By aiming to achieve goals, children have a greater sense of control over what they are doing and it helps them to focus on achieving something specific. In essence, a goal is something which is identifiable and which one works towards achieving over a specified period of time. For example, a short-term goal might be to complete three maths exercises every weekday, and the long-term goal might be to obtain 65% for maths in the end-of-year examination.

Six steps to successful goal setting
1. **Identify needs.** Decide on a few short- and long-term goals. In other words, help your child decide what he or she wants to achieve and by when. Identify a few goals and write them down. This can be done on a form such as the following:

Date ....

My goal in .... for this

term is to .... I wish

to achieve this goal by ....

with .... % accuracy.

Pupil .... Parent ....

---

2. **Set realistic goals.** Goals should be positive, reasonable and attainable. It is no use setting goals that are impractical or impossible to meet. Continual failure arising from being unable to attain goals destroys self-esteem. Goals should also be flexible: they should not be discarded, but rather re-evaluated and altered to suit the child's updated needs and progress.
3. **Have clear goals.** A more general type of goal can be divided into a set of specific objectives. Objectives clearly state exactly what is to be done. This can be done on a form such as the one given on the next page, for example.

4. **Set time limits.** Each goal should allow a reasonable amount of time for the child to complete the tasks necessary to achieve it.
5. **Monitor progress.** Evaluate and monitor your child's progress and, from time to time, review his or her goals.
6. **Reward accomplishments.** Continually encourage your child to persevere and work towards his or her goals. Acknowledge his or her accomplishments and give praise when he or she achieves a goal, no matter how small.

Name .... Week ....

Subject ....

My goal this week is ....

....

To achieve my goal I will

....

....

....

---

17. Supporting discipline

Good discipline at school and in the home is necessary to encourage and inspire appropriate behaviour, and for the establishment of an environment free of disruptions, in which children can engage in meaningful learning activities. Discipline is not punishment. It is the means by which good behaviour is encouraged and taught, and it should therefore be seen as something positive.

In Chapter 10 we looked at discipline in the school. It was pointed out that parents should be familiar with the school's disciplinary policy and the legal rules governing certain forms of punishment. It is also important for parents to reinforce school discipline by establishing good discipline in the home.

Tips for parents

- Set limits for your child. Establish a clear set of rules and a code of behaviour for your child at home. Let your child know what you expect from him or her and the consequences of unacceptable behaviour.
- Become familiar with the school and classroom rules and codes of behaviour.
- Support teachers by upholding their discipline when it is reasonable and fair.
- Avoid being too hasty in defending your child and taking sides without first checking the facts. If your child feels he or she has been unfairly punished, discuss the situation with the teacher in order to get all the facts.
- Do not immediately rush off to the school since this creates a negative impresson and undermines the authority of the teacher and the school. If you have a particular problem, rather discuss the matter with the principal or the teacher concerned.

Punishment

Punishment can often do more harm than good. Sometimes it merely reinforces the very behaviour you are trying to correct. If misbehaving is the only for way the child to get attention, punishment will only serve to reinforce low self-esteem and simply makes matters worse. Experts in the field of psychology and education maintain that punishment works best in settings where positive behaviour is acknowledged and reinforced.

The following strategies are widely recommended:
- Match the punishment to the problem
- Avoid punishing in the heat of the moment
- Make sure the child knows why he or she is being punished
- Be clear about what behaviour you consider to be acceptable
- Do not make empty threats
- Support your words with action
- Avoid using sarcasm
- Be firm, decisive and consistent
- Forgive and forget. Do not stay angry for too long
- Stay calm when handing out punishment.

Strategies for encouraging positive discipline

Positive discipline can be encouraged by means of the following strategies.

Setting rules
Define limits and a clear set of rules, and enforce them. There should only be a few rules, but they should be realistic and consistently applied. Rules should also be flexible so that they can be modified according to circumstances. Discuss the rules with your child and let him or her help decide on some of them. The consequences of breaking the rules should also be explained so that your child knows exactly what to expect. Present the consequences as choices — in other words, he or she can choose whether to misbehave and accept the consequences, or to behave and avoid conflict.

Time out
At times it is useful to remove the child from the situation which is giving rise to the behaviour problem. This helps to diffuse the situation. For example, the child might be sent to his or her bedroom or into another room until he or she has calmed down and can talk about the problem rationally. To make time out effective, it is important to leave the child alone for only a short period before discussing the matter and resolving the conflict.

Removal of privileges

Children should be fully aware of the consequences of poor behaviour. Identify certain privileges that can be withdrawn temporarily as a means of punishment, such as not being allowed to ride his or her bike, not being allowed to have a friend over to play over a weekend, or not being allowed to watch television.

Responsibilities

Giving your child responsibility, such as seeing that certain chores are done, is one way of encouraging good discipline. Having responsibility gives children a sense of self-worth and makes them feel useful, even if at first they object to some of the less enjoyable responsibilities, like keeping their bedrooms tidy, washing the dishes, setting the table for dinner, or other domestic chores.

Problem-solving

The problem-solving approach is usually more effective with older children. Using the problem-solving approach requires you to identify the problem and determine the circumstances giving rise to it. Consider the different positive ways in which the problem can be resolved. Select one of the options and develop a plan of action. It is imperative that both parent and child are involved in the problem-solving process.

Rewarding good behaviour

A positive way of encouraging good behaviour is to reward children when they behave well. Rewards serve to reinforce and promote acceptable behaviour. Effective praise, as discussed in the previous chapter, will also encourage children to behave well. Let your child know that you recognise his or her good behaviour.

18. Homework without tears

Homework, which is an extension of work done at school, is an essential part of your child's schooling. It is, however, probably the least-liked activity! Homework does not need to be boring or a kind of drudgery for parents and children, provided there is understanding and co-operation between parents, pupils and teachers.

Is homework necessary?

There are many good reasons why children should do homework. Homework is valuable because it:
• instils good discipline;
• develops a sense of responsibility;
• fosters children's creativity;
• reinforces learning experiences;
• helps to achieve learning objectives;
• is a good indication of whether the child has understood the work done in class;
• develops good study habits;
• provides an opportunity to practise skills; and
• shows parents what their children are doing at school.

However, homework, should not:
• be set simply for the sake of setting it;
• be used as a form of punishment;
• consist of entirely new work;
• be set just for pupils who are having difficulty with their work;
• be beyond the child's capabilities;
• be used for merely completing work that has not been finished in class; or
• be of such a nature that parents have to do the work for their children.

How much time should be spent on homework?

Education departments usually recommend a certain amount of time for homework according to the child's age and standard. This information should be available to parents in the school prospectus, a handbook for parents or in a homework policy. Make sure that you obtain this information at the beginning of each school year.

The following are examples of the amount of time allocated to homework.

Grade 1 – Standard 1
During this phase homework should be an opportunity to practise skills that have been learned at school. Children should not be given new work or work unrelated to the day's classroom activities. In Standard 1 some written work can be set for practising basic writing skills.

Reading is a very important activity. Children should be given ample opportunity to read for enjoyment. Refer to Chapter 20 for more ideas on reading with your child.

Senior primary phase
The minimum amount of time for homework set for each standard is given as follows:
Standard 2: $\frac{1}{2}$ hour
Standard 3: $\frac{1}{2}$ hour
Standard 4: $\frac{3}{4}$ hour

Junior secondary phase
Standard 5: 1 hour
Standard 6: 1 $\frac{1}{2}$ hours
Standard 7: 2 hours

Senior secondary phase
Standard 8: 2 $\frac{1}{2}$ hours
Standard 9: 3 hours
Standard 10: 4 hours

What parents ought to know about their child's homework

At the beginning of each year it is advisable to obtain the following information from the school:
• homework rules/policy;
• materials needed, e.g. homework diary;
• day(s) on which homework for specific subjects is given;
• amount of time to be allocated (see above); and
• what is expected of parents.

Tips for helping your child with homework

- Sit down with your child and plan a schedule for completing homework tasks.
- Help your child choose a suitable place for doing homework.
- Encourage your child to work on his or her own.
- Provide help and encouragement but do not do the homework for your child.
- Give constructive praise for homework completed.
- Sign the homework diary every day.
- Keep in regular contact with your child's teacher(s).
- Read and discuss the homework tasks with your child.
- Encourage your child to join a public library.
- Talk to your child about subjects that interest him or her.
- Limit television viewing of non-educational programmes. Suggest alternative activities if the weather is fine, such as games outside.
- Help your child gather information for projects and homework tasks.
- Make sure that your child has the basic materials to complete homework assignments, e.g. pens, ruler, eraser, sharpener, pencils and coloured pencils.
- Be sensitive to problems experienced by your child.
- Monitor homework regularly. Children should not be overloaded with homework. Younger children, in particular, should have sufficient time to play or watch television in the afternoon.

Incomplete homework

If children do not complete their homework and hand it in on time they are often punished. If your child genuinely cannot do a particular homework assignment, or if it cannot be completed within a reasonable period of time, write a note to the teacher in the homework diary next to the item. Do not merely sign the diary as if the homework has been completed. Encourage your child to discuss his or her problem with the teacher before the start of the lesson and to explain why the homework was not completed. If your child waits for the teacher to collect the work or if it goes unmentioned, the teacher is likely to punish him or her for not doing the homework. This merely aggravates the situation.

Homework contracts

Homework contracts are a way of helping your child to plan his or her homework and to complete it on time. Homework contracts are particularly useful for children who forget their homework books at school or at home, or who take too long to complete tasks. The homework contracts can be drawn up by the parent or the teacher together with the child.

The examples which follow can be used to draw up a contract. Also make use of the reproducible pages at the end of this guide. If such a contract is used, it is very important to follow up on the work to be completed and to check the work when it is due. Remember to praise your child for work that is complete and properly done.

Example 1

My homework

Date ....

Task ....

....

To be completed by ....

Signed

Pupil .... Teacher ....

Example 2

Homework Tasks

Subject ....

Tasks to be completed   Due date

1. ....

2. ....

3. ....

4. ....

Signed

Pupil ....   Teacher ....

Suggestions for coping with homework problems

Various problems may crop up with regard to homework. The following paragraphs contain suggestions for dealing with those which are most often encountered.

What should I do when my child takes too long to complete homework tasks?
- Check your child's diary well in advance.
- Try and find out from his or her teachers what work is due on what days, if this is not clearly indicated in the homework diary.
- Together with your child, decide on a practical homework timetable.
- Write out the schedule and display it prominently so that you are reminded when homework is due.
- Help your child gather the information that he or she needs well in advance. Get help from friends and family if required.
- Reward your child for work that is done on time.

What should I do if my child refuses to do the work?
- Discuss the homework task(s) with your child and try to establish the reason why he or she refuses to do it.

- If the work is too difficult or there is too much to complete, discuss the problem with the teacher and work out a plan for solving the problem.
- Your child should also understand the consequences of not doing the homework, especially if he or she is just being difficult. He or she should understand that punishment may be forthcoming both at home and at school. Children need to learn responsibility and the value of doing homework.
- A homework contract is a useful strategy for dealing with this kind of problem.

What can I do if my own work prevents me from supervising my child's homework?
- Work out a homework schedule for your child to follow each afternoon while you are at work.
- Discuss your child's homework needs and requirements with the person who supervises him or her.
- If possible, take time to telephone your child before he or she starts the homework.
- If you are not at home, your child must realise that he or she is responsible for doing homework and that you expect it to be completed by the time you get home, especially if you get home late.
- When you get home, check to see what work has been done, talk about it and sign the homework diary if you are satisfied. This need not take much time.

19. Helpful study hints

Examinations and class tests are a very important part of your child's school programme. Tests are usually set on a regular basis and many schools have weekly tests or cycle tests for which children need to prepare. However, children often fail tests or obtain low marks because they do not know how to study and because studying is not a regular part of their programme after school hours. Teachers and parents often take it for granted that children know how to learn, to read with meaning, to take notes, to summarise, to organise their work, to recall facts and to use a textbook – all of which are essential study skills.

How to help your child study

Study time should come after written homework has been completed. It should be a time to review, revise, practise and memorise work. Children should be encouraged to get into the habit of revising work on a regular basis and not merely the day before the test. There are many ways in which you can help your child to study effectively.

Find a suitable place to study
To study effectively your child will need to have a quiet place for private study. This need not take up a great deal of space, as long as he or she knows that for a certain period of time that space is his or hers to study in, and that he or she will not be disturbed unnecessarily while sitting there. Encourage brothers and sisters to co-operate and respect each other's need for peace and quiet during study time.

Set a regular time aside each day for studying
Encourage your child to study at more or less the same time each day. This will help to establish a routine and will encourage self-discipline. It will also help ensure that studying is not left to the last minute. If children have not been set specific homework they often think that they need not do any homework at all. They may not have written homework or homework for the very next day, but they can always find some work to revise or reading to do.

Supervision

Try to supervise your child's study programme on a regular basis. Encourage the child to talk about what he or she is studying and ask questions. Use every opportunity to let him or her tell you what he or she has learned, as this will help to recall the work and organise his or her thoughts.

Equipment

Make sure that all the necessary equipment, such as paper, pens, pencils, coloured pencils, sharpener, dictionary and perhaps even a thesaurus, are available. It is not necessary to buy all these items at once. You can also suggest to family and friends that they give these as gifts on special occasions.

Study methods

There are many different ways in which to study and children do not all learn in the same way or use the same study methods.

Children are given some instruction on study methods at school, but this is not done on a regular basis. If you are concerned about your child's study habits, discuss the matter with the teacher.

Your child may take the following steps for a more effective method of studying:

Step 1: Go over the work that is to be studied.

Step 2: Organise the work into manageable sections. Often children fail to learn because they are overwhelmed by the quantity and do not know where to start.

Step 3: Arrange for there to be enough time to cover all the sections. Write out a timetable. Set realistic goals.

Step 4: Choose a suitable study method. The following method is a good example:

- Study all the notes and questions that are given.
- Read through the section of work carefully.
- Make brief notes by writing down key words and phrases. List important facts and events.
- Make a list of questions. Rewrite headings and subheadings as questions.
- Close the book and recall what has been read. Answer the questions.
- Review the notes. Check the answers against the notes. Fill in missing information.

Using diagrams

Diagrams are a useful visual way of organising and summarising notes. Mapping is a visual representation of information that clearly indicates relationships. In mapping, the main idea or concept (key word) is placed in the centre of the diagram and the important information relating to that concept is placed around the concept.

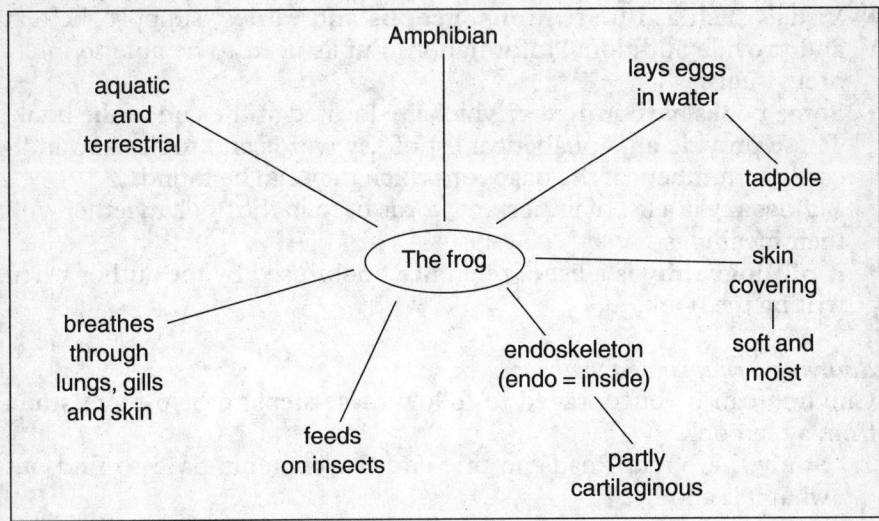

How to use a textbook

Besides notes and worksheets which have been prepared by the teacher, the textbook is still the most important source of information, especially in high school. Not all textbooks are easy to read and understand, however. Moreover, teachers and parents tend to take for granted that children know how to use a textbook. Children are seldom taught how to use a textbook, yet good textbook skills can improve children's grades dramatically. Knowing how to use a textbook properly also helps children to find information more easily.

Important features of a textbook
When children are taught how to use a textbook they should be made aware of the different features. This information is valuable for helping them to find information for essays, reports and projects.
• The **title page** shows the title of the book and gives the name(s) of the author(s) and publisher.

- The **table of contents** outlines the structure of the book and lists the topics dealt with in the book.
- The **preface** is an introduction to the book. It gives important information about the aim of the book and the viewpoints of the author(s).
- A book is divided into **chapters**. Each chapter deals with a particular topic. It is not always necessary to read an entire book to obtain required information. Relevant chapters can be selected.
- Visuals such as **illustrations**, **graphs** and **tables**, support the text and provide additional information. Pupils need to be able to interpret visuals.
- Some books have **indexes**, which are located at the end of the book. These provide an alphabetical list of key words and topics and indicate the numbers of the pages on which they can be found.
- A **glossary** is a list of important words used in the book together with their meanings.
- A **bibliography** is a list of reference books used by the author when writing the book.

Studying a chapter of a textbook
Children can be encouraged to follow these steps to help them study from a textbook.
1. Study the book. Read the title and the contents page to find out what it is about.

2. Look through the chapter to be studied.
   • Read the headings and subheadings.
   • Read the introduction at the beginning, and the summary at the end.
   • Read through the study questions.
   • Look at all the diagrams and illustrations.
3. Read the chapter.
   • Write down key words and phrases.
   • Write down unfamiliar words.
   • Write down important names and dates.
   • Write down important definitions.
4. Recall information.
   • Close the book and summarise aloud, in your own words, what has been read.
   • Answer the study questions.
5. Review the chapter.
   • Read the chapter again to make sure that the content has been understood.

20. How to improve your child's reading and writing skills

Reading with confidence

Reading is essential for success at school. In order to understand all school subjects and school work, children need to be able to read. Although schools do not expect parents to teach their children to read – in fact many teachers prefer parents not to – parents can help their children improve their reading. Research suggests that parents who read with their children contribute towards an improvement in their school performance. Reading with children should not be limited to the junior primary phase, but should extend throughout the primary and secondary phases.

Tips for improving reading

- Provide books and magazines for your child to read. This need not be a costly exercise. Reading material can be obtained from the local library, friends, family and second-hand bookshops.
- Read to your child and let him or her read to you and talk about the story and/or information found in the book.
- Parents of high school children can read their children's setwork books, that is, the literature books which the children are required to read and study. If you are unable to read these books, try to obtain recordings and listen to the story. You will then be able to discuss the book with your child.
- Encourage your child to use the local library. Make time to go to the library with him or her and choose books together.
- Play vocabulary and spelling games with your child.
- Do crossword puzzles together. Encourage your child to make up his or her own crossword puzzles for the family to do.
- Encourage your child to use a dictionary.
- Let your child read aloud to you or another adult.

Reading with young children

Parents who read with their children are helping to improve their child's performance at school. Reading regularly with children helps to

develop their vocabulary and language skills. "Reading for meaning" is necessary to ensure that the child understands what he or she is reading. Sometimes children will read a story perfectly but when questioned, you discover they have not understood what they have read! "Reading for meaning" involves asking questions about the book and explaining words and phrases. Try not to interrupt the child too often because this spoils the flow of the story and makes comprehension more difficult.

Here are some suggestions for reading aloud with your child:

- Set aside a regular time each day – fifteen minutes will be sufficient.
- Sit next to your child. Let him or her hold the book and turn the pages.
- Look at the pictures together and discuss them.
- You can extend your child's vocabulary and language by explaining unfamiliar words and sentences.
- At the end of the story, ask your child questions. You could ask which parts of the book he or she enjoyed, and which character he or she liked the most.

20.4 Successful writing

Writing is an essential means of communication, and forms a major part of the learning process. Writing is a means of communicating ideas, sharing information, expressing thoughts and imparting knowledge. Children spend a substantial part of the school day engaged in a variety of writing activities. Each subject requires a different style of writing and involves specialised terminology which children must understand before they can learn the content of the subject. For example, writing a history essay, writing up a science experiment and compiling a biology report, all require different styles of writing and different vocabulary.

Children should start learning these skills as early as the junior primary level. For example, for creative writing they may be asked to write about a windy day, and in the nature study lesson they may be asked to label a tree, which means they must be able to give the correct names for the different parts of the tree. As the child moves up to the higher standards, the writing skills become more difficult and complex.

Successful writers ...
• write logically;
• use suitable language;
• use an appropriate kind of writing style;
• use correct spelling, punctuation and grammar;
• express ideas clearly.

What does writing involve?

Writing is not an easy task. Developing and practising writing skills is therefore very important for writing successfully. Writing is not a skill that, once acquired, needs no further effort. Writing is a *process* that should be practised often and continuously developed and improved.

The writing process involves pre-writing activities, drafting, revising, editing and proofreading. When your child has a writing activity for homework, encourage and help him or her to work through these different stages. At first he or she might think this is time-consuming and tiresome, but the end result will be rewarding.

• **Pre-writing activities.** During the pre-writing stage, children are given the opportunity to discuss the writing activity before they start. Discuss the task with your child and help him or her to gather information and think about what he or she is going to write. If necessary, make some suggestions.
• **Drafting.** At this stage children plan what they are going to write and write their first draft. It is not necessary to place too much stress on neatness and correct language. Encourage your child to write quickly and spontaneously.

- **Reviewing and revising.** When the writing activity is complete, children are given the opportunity to discuss what they have written and to obtain feedback on the content and language. They can use this information to rewrite and improve the first draft.
- **Editing.** Children should be taught to edit their own work. Editing helps the writer to recognise his or her own mistakes and make corrections. To be able to edit their own work, children need to be taught the skills of editing, such as combining sentences, eliminating unnecessary words and phrases, using correct punctuation, and organising information in a logical way. This is particularly important for high school pupils who are required to write lengthy essays and reports. Children should also be encouraged to edit one another's work, as well. When the draft has been reviewed and edited, the final copy can be written.
- **Proofreading.** When the final copy has been written, children should read it over again and then proofread it carefully to check for errors. At this stage the errors should be minimal.

Publishing children's work

Displaying and publishing children's written work are two ways in which to motivate, reward and share children's writing. There are various ways in which this can be achieved. Children's work can be displayed in the classroom and at home. Alternatively, it can be published in the school magazine or other children's literary journals. Children can also be encouraged to make their own books.

Tips for helping your child to develop writing skills

Here are some ideas you can try out if you want to help your child become a successful writer:
- Encourage your child to write notes and letters to friends and family members.
- Encourage your child to write down messages accurately.
- Encourage your child to write his or her own stories, poems and short plays. These pieces of writing can be kept in a personal writing folder.
- Encourage your child to write stories, poems and factual items for the school magazine.
- Provide your child with a variety of writing materials. These can be given as gifts.
- Ask your child to write out the family shopping list.

- Encourage your child to read and write about subjects in which he or she is interested.
- Praise writing that has been done at school.
- Pay attention to content and not only to spelling and grammar.
- Encourage neat writing but don't be over-critical because this can stifle creativity and spontaneity.
- Expose your child to a variety of reading materials which serve as examples of good writing models.

Appendix A – Useful addresses

Centre for Dyslexia
P O Box 31186
0134 Totiusdal
Tel. 012 – 326-2570

The centre provides professional advice, testing and educational programmes to parents of children with dyslexia and related problems.

Education Information Centre
Khotso House
62 Marshall Street
2107 Marshalltown
Tel. 011 -

The centre provides information on careers and bursaries.

Educational Institute for Day Care Centres
P O Box 192
2000 Johannesburg
Tel. 011 – 337-6673

Johannesburg College of Education
Extracurricular Centre for Gifted Children
27 St Andrews Road
2193 Parktown
Tel. 011 – 484-7966

Rebecca Ostrowiak School of Reading
5 Selkirk Street
1401 Germiston
Tel. 011 – 873-1012

This school provides a wide variety of reading and study programmes for children and adults. It also has a home-reading programme.

South African Council on Alcoholism & Drug Dependence
318 Happiness House
2001 Johannesburg
Tel. 011 – 725-5810

Southern African Association for Early Childhood Educare
P O Box 673
0001 Pretoria
Tel. 012 – 322-0601

This Association can provide useful information and advice on pre-school education. Depending on the information required, the Association has a number of regional offices to which queries will be directed.

The Parent and Child Counselling Centre
32 Honey Street
Berea
Tel. – 484-1734

The centre provides counselling to parents of children with social and emotional problems.

The Remedial Teaching Foundation
P O Box 2844
2000 Johannesburg
Tel. 011 – 29-2201

The South African Association of Learning and Educational disabilities
c/o Department of Specialised Education
University of Witwatersrand
2001 Wits
Tel. 011 – 716-5287

Pages 101 to 106 are reproducible pages for use by parents and children.

Choosing a school

1. Is the school conveniently situated?
2. What public transport is available?
3. Are school fees compulsory and how much are they?
4. How many pupils are there in the school? (What is the school's enrolment?)
5. What is the ratio of pupils to teachers?
6. Is the school co-educational?
7. Is the school multiracial?
8. Does the school offer the subjects your child requires?
9. Are the academic standards of the school satisfactory?
10. Is the school staffed by well-qualified teachers?
11. What is the language medium of instruction? Will your child cope with the language required?
12. Does the school offer academic support programmes?
13. Does the school have adequate academic and non-academic facilities, such as a science laboratory, media centre, playground and sports fields?
14. Does the extracurricular programme include activities in which your child is interested?
15. Does the school have a students' representative council?
16. What is the school's policy on religious education? Does the school subscribe to or encourage a specific religion? If so, what provision is made for children of other religions?
17. Is the discipline of the school satisfactory? Is there a clearly stated code of conduct?
18. Does the school provide after-school care? Are there study centres?
19. Does the school have hostel (boarding) facilities?
20. Do the values and standards of the school fit in with your own beliefs?

IMPORTANT SCHOOL DATA

Name of school

....

School address

....
....
....
....

Phone numbers

....
....

Name of secretary

....

Name of chairman of governing body

....

Name of class/form teacher

....

Names of subject teachers

....
....
....
....
....
....
....

Deatils of school times

....
....

PERSONAL HOMEWORK PLAN

TASK   DUE DATE

....
....
....
....
....
....
....
....
....
....
....
....
....
....
....
....

WEEKLY HOMEWORK PLAN

Monday

....

....

....

Tuesday

....

....

....

Wednesday

....

....

....

Thursday

....

....

....

Friday

....

....

....

HOMEWORK CONTRACT

Date: ....

I am having difficulty with ....

....

I will do the following:

1. ....

2. ....

3. ....

4. ....

5. ....

I undertake to complete these tasks by ....

Signed

....	....	....
Pupil	Teacher	Parent

CHECKLIST FOR STUDYING A CHAPTER OF A TEXTBOOK

HAVE YOU ....

– studied the chapter? ....

– read the introduction? ....

– read the summary? ....

– read the study questions? ....

– read the headings and subheadings? ....

– noted key words and phrases? ....

– found the meanings of unfamiliar words? ....

– answered the study questions? ....

– reviewed the chapter? ....

Bibliography

Bondesio, M.J., Beckmann, J.L., Oosthuizen, I.J., Prinsloo, J.G. and Van Wyk, J.G. (1989): *The teaching profession:legal requirements*. Pretoria: Van der Walt.

Bray, W., Van Wuk, J.G. and Oosthuizen, I.J. (1989): *Case law on education*. Durban: Butterworth.

Buchel, A.J. (1992): *Practical school management*. Pretoria: Acacia.

Canter, L and Canter, M. (1991): *Parents on your side*. Santa Monica: Lee Canter and Associates.

Curtis, A.M. (1993): *A curriculum for the pre-school child*. London: Routledge.

Department of Education and Culture. *Manual for Model C schools*.

Department of Education and Training (1990): *Manual for school organisation*. Pretoria, DET.

Dwyer, B. (1989): *Parents, teachers and partners*. Rozelle: Primary English Teaching Association.

Edwards, V. and Redfern, A. (1988): *At home in school*. London: Routledge.

EIC (1992): *Bursary Register*. Johannesburg: Education Information Centre.

Ferguson, S. and Mazin, L. (1989): *Parent power. A programme to help your child succeed at school*. New York: Clarkson N. Potter.

Fredericks, A.D. and Rasinski, T.V. (1990): "Working with parents. Involving the uninvolved:how to." *The Reading Teacher*, February 1990: 424-425.

Gallagher, J.J. (1985): *Teaching the gifted child*. Boston: Allyn and Bacon.

Government Gazette No. 12381. No. R.690 30 March 1990. Regulations relating to school management councils of public schools.

Government Gazette No. 12381. No. R.704 30 March 1990. Regulations relating to the control of pupils, suspension and expulsion of pupils from, and meting out punishments to pupils in public, state and state-aided schools.

Hallahan, D.P. and Kauffmann, J.M. (1991): *Exceptional children*. Boston: Allyn and Bacon.

Kaplinsky, S. (1992): *Preparing for a quality matric. A five year plan for parents, scholars and teachers*. Cape Town: Don Nelson.

Lemmer, E.L. and Squelch, J.M. (1993): *Multicultural education. A teachers' manual.* Johannesburg: Southern Books.

Long, R. (1986) *Developing parent involvement in primary schools.* London: Macmillan.

Macbeth, A. (1989): *Involving parents. Effective parent-teacher relations.* Oxford: Heinemann.

Maring, G.H. and Magelky, J. (1990): "Working with parents. Effective communication: key to parent/community involvement." *The Reading Teacher,* April 606-607.

Munn, P. (1993): *Parents and schools. Customers, managers or partners?* London: Routledge.

Prinsloo, J.G. and Beckmann, J.L. (1988): *Education and the rights and duties of parents, teachers and children.* Johanneburg: Lex Patria.

Rasinski, T. and Fredericks, A.D. (1989): "Working with parents. Can parents make a difference?" *The Reading teacher,* October: 84-85.

Shalaway, L. (1989): *Learning to teach.* Cleveland: Edgell Communications.

South Africa. Department of Education and Training Act 90 of 1979.

South Africa. Education Affairs Act (House of Assembly) Act 70 of 1988.

South Africa. National Policy for General Education Affairs Act, No. 76 of 1984.

Stacey, M. (1991): *Parents and teachers together.* Milton Keynes: Oxford University Press.

Sutherland, M. (1988): *Theory of education.* London: Longman.

Taylor, F. (1986): *Parents' rights in education.* Essex: Longman

Transvaal Education Department (1993): *Manual for school organisation.* Pretoria: TED.

Van Wyk, J.G. (1991): *The law of education for the teacher.* Pretoria: Academica.

Wolfendale, S. (1992): *Empowering parents and teachers. Working for children.* London: Cassell.

Wallace, B. (1983): *Teaching the very able child.* London: Ward Lock Educational Ltd.